THE
PASSION
TRANSLATION

D1111723

Matthew

OUR
LOVING
KING

Translated from Greek and Aramaic Texts

DR. BRIAN SIMMONS

tPt
BIBLE

BroadStreet
PUBLISHING

Matthew: Our Loving King, The Passion Translation®
Translated directly from the original Greek and Aramaic texts by Dr. Brian Simmons

Published by BroadStreet Publishing Group, LLC
Racine, Wisconsin, USA
www.broadstreetpublishing.com

© 2014 The Passion Translation®

ISBN-13: 978-1-4245-4971-9 (paperback)
ISBN-13: 978-1-4245-4972-6 (e-book)

Cover and interior design by Garborg Design Works, Inc. | www.garborgdesign.com
Interior typesetting by Katherine Lloyd | www.theDESKonline.com

Printed in the United States of America

14 15 16 17 18 19 20   10 9 8 7 6 5 4 3 2 1

Translator's Introduction to Matthew

AT A GLANCE

Author: Matthew, the former Jewish tax collector and disciple of Jesus

Audience: Originally, the Jewish Christian church and the Jewish people

Date: AD 55–80

Type of Literature: Ancient historical biography

Major Themes: Gospel-telling, Old Testament fulfillment, heaven's kingdom realm, kingdom-realm living

Outline:

Jesus' Birth and Ministry Preparation — 1:1–4:11
Jesus Teaches His Kingdom Realm — 4:12–7:29
Jesus Demonstrates His Kingdom Realm — 8:1–11:1
Jesus Is Opposed — 11:2–13:53
Jesus Disciples His Disciples — 13:54–18:35
Jesus Marches to the Cross — 19:1–25:46
Jesus Dies, Rises, and Sends — 26:1–28:20

ABOUT MATTHEW

Four centuries of silence. Where was the promised Messiah? The Jewish people were waiting for the word of the prophets to come true, for they had prophesied that he would come. Then suddenly, the angel Gabriel made an appearance to a teenage girl to announce his birth. Shepherds saw a brilliant angelic light show on the hillside.

Wise men went out in search of him.
The light of the star shined over his manger.
Insecure Herod wanted to kill him.
Satan cruelly tested him.
The prophet John presented him to Israel.
God anointed him with the power of the Holy Spirit.

Then one day the King came into the Jewish meeting house and announced: "I'm here! I've come to set you free and to wash away sins, and liberate those who love and follow me."

We can thank God for Matthew, for in his gospel he presents our eternal King. Matthew means "gift of Yahweh," and he lives up to his name. Thank you, Matthew, for the gift of your life and for what you have left for us in your gospel!

PURPOSE

Matthew is a natural bridge between the Old Testament and the New because it has the most Jewish character. From the first verse to the last, Matthew establishes Jesus as a direct descendant of King David, preserving and fulfilling his royal line as the rightful heir as well as a descendant of Abraham, the father of Israel.

Furthermore, Matthew portrays Jesus as the new and greater Moses, who not only upholds the Jewish Torah but intensifies it—not in a legalistic way, but in a spiritual way, because following his teachings is the way into his heavenly kingdom realm.

It would be a mistake, however, to say there is only one purpose for this book. While one primary purpose is to communicate the Jesus story to the Jewish people, Matthew also means to communicate Jesus' story to us. One particular aspect of the Jesus story that Matthew wants to share is that Jesus is King of a heavenly kingdom realm. Mark and Luke also speak of God's kingdom realm, but Matthew focuses on how people behave as citizens of that realm, with Jesus as their loving King.

AUTHOR AND AUDIENCE

It is believed that Matthew may have been the first apostle to write a gospel, and he possibly wrote it in Hebrew (Aramaic). Though some maintain that Matthew wrote his gospel after the destruction of the temple in AD 70, it's possible he wrote it anywhere between AD 55 to the mid-60s. He was a wealthy tax collector who profited greatly from his duty of representing Rome. And then one day, the Man from Galilee stood in front of him and said, "Come, follow me."

There continues to be debate over the original language of Matthew's account. In AD 170 Eusebius quoted Irenaeus as saying, "Matthew published his gospel among the Hebrews in their own language, while Peter and Paul in Rome were preaching and founding the church."[a] This, along with numerous other quotations from church fathers (Origen, Jerome, Augustine) would mean that the original manuscript of Matthew's gospel was written in Hebrew. Regardless, it is without dispute that Matthew was a Jewish man who presents a Jewish King who now sits on the throne of glory for all people.

Perhaps an unbiased look at the Hebrew and Aramaic manuscripts would yield further nuances of our Jewish heritage as believers in Yeshua

---

a Eusebius, *Historia Ecclesiastica* III. 24.5–6 and V. 8, 2.

and would strengthen our understanding of the inspired Scriptures. You will find ample footnotes throughout this translation to assist you in your study.

MAJOR THEMES

Gospel-Telling. The word *gospel* doesn't simply mean "good news." It is derived from the Greek verb *euangelizomai,* which means "to preach the good news." In other words, Matthew is writing to tell us heaven's truths embedded in the earthly events of the Man Jesus. Matthew isn't giving us dry theology, but sharing stories and teachings designed in such a way as to unfold the majestic, magisterial person of Jesus, who embodies all of our theologies!

Old Testament. As the first book of the New Testament, Matthew connects the past with the present and with the future. He quotes sixty times from the Old Testament, showing us that the New was enfolded in the Old, while the New Testament is the Old Testament unfolded and explained. The Old Testament is more central in Matthew than in any other gospel, both in frequency and in emphasis. If the Jewish story is always pointing forward, Matthew's gospel is its final act. It brings resolution to the Old Testament by presenting King Jesus and His kingdom realm and community as fulfilling their prophetic expectations.

Parables. There are unique components to Matthew's gospel. For example, he records extensively the allegorical teachings of Jesus known as parables. Twelve are detailed by Matthew, and nine of them are unique to this account. He gives us two miracles of Jesus that are found nowhere else: the healing of two blind men and the miracle coin found in the fish's mouth. It is through these simple stories that the nature of both our King and his kingdom really come to life!

Heavenly Kingdom Realm. Matthew brings us the realm of the heavenly kingdom and sets its virtue and reality before us. The phrase "kingdom realm" is used nearly forty times as Jesus offers it to you and me. And Jesus is described as the King fourteen times. This is the gospel of the King and his kingdom, but a different kingdom than even his followers expected. For the kingdom realm that Jesus ushered in would not liberate the Jewish people from oppression from the Roman government as they expected—we can define neither the King nor his kingdom ourselves. Instead, he offers not only Jews but every person access to an eternal, heavenly realm free from the consequences of sin and an oasis to refresh our lives!

Kingdom-Realm Living. Matthew's gospel isn't only about our loving King and his kingdom, it's also about his subjects who act and live within that kingdom. The church is the community of Christ's heavenly kingdom realm, and Jesus' sermon on the hillside is the final Torah of the kingdom realm. For Matthew, a godly lover (the "righteous") is someone who has chosen to submit to Jesus as King and whose life is lived in accordance with his ethics.

A WORD ABOUT THE PASSION TRANSLATION

The message of God's story is timeless; the Word of God doesn't change. But the methods by which that story is communicated should be timely; the vessels that steward God's Word can and should change.

One of those timely methods and vessels is Bible translation. Bible translations are both a gift and a problem. They give us the words God spoke through his servants, but words can be very poor containers for revelation because they leak! The meanings of words change from one generation to the next. Meaning is influenced by culture, background, and a thousand other details. You can imagine how differently the Hebrew authors of the Old Testament saw the world three thousand years ago.

There is no such thing as a truly literal translation of the Bible, for there is not an equivalent language that perfectly conveys the meaning of the biblical text except as it is understood in its original cultural and linguistic setting.

Therefore, a translation can be a problem. The problem, however, is solved when we seek to transfer meaning, not merely words, from the original text to the receptor language.

The Passion Translation is a groundbreaking attempt to reintroduce the passion and fire of the Bible to the English reader. It doesn't merely convey the original, literal meaning of words. It expresses God's passion for people and his world by translating the original, life-changing message of God's Word for modern readers.

God longs to have his Word expressed in every language in a way that would unlock the "passion" of his heart. Our goal is to trigger inside every English speaker an overwhelming response to the truth of the Bible, unfiltered by religious jargon. This is a heart-level translation, from the passion of God's heart to the passion of your heart.

We pray and trust that this version of God's Word will kindle in you a burning, passionate desire for him and his heart, while impacting the church for years to come!

—Dr. Brian Simmons

One

From Abraham to Christ

[1] This is the scroll of the lineage and birth[a] of Jesus,[b] the Anointed One, the descendant of both David and Abraham.

[2] Abraham had a son named Isaac, who had a son named Jacob, who had a son named Judah (he and his brothers became the tribes of Israel).[c]

[3] Judah and Tamar[d] had twin sons, Perez and Hezron. Perez had a son named Hezron, who had a son named Ram, [4]who had a son named Amminadab, who had a son named Nashon, [5]who had a son named Salmon, who, along with Rahab, had a son named Boaz. Boaz and Ruth had a son named Obed, who was the father of Jesse, [6]and Jesse had a son named David, who became the king.[e]

[7] Then David and Bathsheba[f] had a son named Solomon, who had a son named Rehoboam, who had a son named Abijah, who had a son named Asa, [8]who had a son named Jehoshaphat, who had a son named Joram, who had a son named Uzziah, [9]who had a son named Jotham, who had a son named Ahaz, who had a son named Hezekiah, [10]who had a son named

---

a 1:1 Or "the book of the origin (genesis) of Jesus Christ." The Son of God is eternal and had no beginning (John 1:1; 1 John 1:1). The entire book of Matthew presents the beginning of the glorious story of Jesus, God's Anointed One. The genealogy given by Matthew presents the legal claim of Jesus to be King through the lineage of David from Joseph all the way back to the promises given to Abraham. Luke's account gives the genealogy of Jesus from Mary's lineage through David all the way back to Adam.

b 1:1 The Hebrew name for Jesus is Yeshua (or Y'hoshua) and means "Yahweh is salvation."

c 1:2 Implied in the text.

d 1:3 Matthew includes four women in this genealogy: Tamar, Rahab, Ruth, and Bathsheba.

e 1:6 Implied in the text.

f 1:7 Or "the wife of Uriah."

Manasseh, who had a son named Amos,[a] who had a son named Josiah, [11]who was the father of Jeconiah.[b]

It was during the days of Jeconiah and his brothers that Israel was taken captive and deported to Babylon. [12]About the time of their captivity in Babylon, Jeconiah had a son named Shealtiel, who had a son named Zerubbabel, [13]who had a son named Abiud, who had a son named Eliakim, [14]who had a son named Azor, who had a son named Zadok, who had a son named Achim, who had a son named Eliud, [15]who had a son named Eleazar, who had a son named Matthan, who had a son named Jacob, [16]who was the father of Joseph, the husband[c] of Mary the mother of Jesus, who is called "the Anointed One."

[17]So from Abraham to David were fourteen generations, and from David to the Babylonian captivity, fourteen generation, and from the Babylonian captivity to Christ, fourteen generations.[d]

An Angel Comes to Joseph

[18]This was how Jesus, God's Anointed One, was born.

His mother, Mary, had promised Joseph to be his wife,[e] but while she

---

a 1:10 Or "Amon."

b 1:11 In Jeremiah 22:24–30 God pronounced a curse on Jeconiah's family line, declaring that they were ineligible to sit on the throne as kings. However, Luke's genealogy goes through David to Mary via Nathan, not Solomon, thus bypassing the curse of Jeconiah's lineage. Matthew's genealogy is meant to establish the legal right of Jesus Christ to be king. So Joseph, as Jesus' adoptive father, passes the right of David's throne legally to Jesus and avoids the curse of Jeconiah through Mary's ancestry. Jesus is the Son of God paternally, and the Son of David maternally through Heli, Mary's father. From the beginning God said that the coming Savior would be the "seed of the woman." See Genesis 3:15 and Galatians 4:4.

c 1:16 Notice that Joseph is named the husband of Mary, not the father of Jesus.

d 1:17 This would make a total of forty-two generations from Abraham to Christ. However, when the names are counted, there are only forty-one. There is a missing generation. What could this mean? Jesus gave birth to the forty-second generation when he died on the cross, for out of his side blood and water flowed. Blood and water come forth at birth. The first Adam "birthed" his wife out of his side, and so Jesus gave birth to his bride from his wounded side. Jesus wants to reproduce himself in us. His last name is not Christ. Christ is the title that explains who he is. He is the Anointed One. "Christ" is also now a corporate body, the body of Christ. We, as the body of Christ, are also anointed ones (Christians). See 1 Corinthians 12:12.

e 1:18 In the Jewish culture the engagement was a prenuptial contract (ketubah), which was entered into before witnesses, that gave legal rights over the girl to the bridegroom. This agreement could only be nullified by going through the formal divorce process. Since the girl still lived with her family, sexual relations were prohibited until after the second event of the public marriage ceremony. This

was still a virgin[a] she became pregnant through the power[b] of the Holy Spirit.[c] [19]Her fiancé, Joseph, was a good man full of integrity and he didn't want to disgrace her, but when he learned of her pregnancy he secretly planned to break the engagement. [20]While he was still debating with himself about what to do,[d] he fell asleep and had a supernatural dream. An angel from the Lord appeared to him in clear light and said, "Joseph, descendant of David, don't hesitate to take Mary into your home as your wife, because the power of the Holy Spirit has conceived a child in her womb. [21]She will give birth to a son and you are to name Him 'Savior,'[e] for He is destined to give His life[f] to save His people from their sins."

[22]This happened so that what the Lord spoke through his prophet would come true:

> [23]**Listen! A virgin[g] will be pregnant,**
> **She will give birth to a Son,**
> **And he will be known as "Emmanuel,"**
> **Which means in Hebrew,**
> **"God became one of us."[h]**

[24]When Joseph awoke from his dream, he did all that the angel of the Lord instructed him to do. He took Mary to be his wife, [25]but they refrained from having sex until she gave birth to her son, whom they named "Jesus."

---

engagement period was usually entered into when the girl turned thirteen. Mary was just a teenager when she gave birth to Jesus.

a 1:18 Or "without them being united (sexually)."

b 1:18 Implied in the text. Although it is the genitive of source, not agency, *the power of the Holy Spirit* is supplied for clarity. See Deuteronomy 20:7 and 22:23–28.

c 1:18 The *Holy Spirit* can also be translated "the Sacred Breath (Spirit-wind)" or "the Spirit of Holiness."

d 1:20 Or "during his inward passion about these things."

e 1:21 Or "Jesus." The Hebrew name for Jesus is Yeshua (or Y'hoshua) and means "Yahweh is salvation, restoration, and deliverance." Implied in the text is that Hebrew (Aramaic) speakers would obviously understand how the name *Yeshua* and *salvation* were linked, reinforcing the theory that Matthew was originally written in Hebrew. This is lost in the Greek word *Iesous* (Jesus).

f 1:21 As translated from the Aramaic.

g 1:23 See also v. 25, which clarifies that Mary was indeed a virgin.

h 1:23 Or "God with us" or "God among us"; that is, God incarnated. See Isaiah 7:14, 8:8, and 8:10 (LXX).

$$Two$$

The Wise Men Visit

[1]Jesus was born in Bethlehem[a] near Jerusalem[b] during the reign of King Herod.[c] After Jesus' birth a group of spiritual priests[d] from the East came to Jerusalem [2]and inquired of the people, "Where is the child who is born king of the Jewish people? We observed his star rising in the sky[e] and we've come to bow before him in worship."

[3]King Herod was shaken to the core when he heard this, and not only him, but all of Jerusalem was disturbed when they heard this news. [4]So he called a meeting of the Jewish ruling priests and religious scholars, demanding that they tell him where the promised Messiah was prophesied to be born.

a 2:1 *Bethlehem*, or *Byt-lehem*, means "house of bread," the prophesied birthplace of Messiah. However, the Hebrew word *lehem* can also mean "fighters." Jesus was born in "the House of Fighters!" This is the city of David, one of the greatest fighters in the entire Bible. Perhaps this is why the people of Jesus' day expected him to fight the Romans and free their land from foreign occupation. Jesus fulfilled both aspects of the meaning of Bethlehem in Gethsemane and on the cross, where he fought the "Goliath" of our souls and won, becoming Bread for the world. God controls all events, proven by the prophecy that Jesus would be born in Bethlehem even though his parents were living in Nazareth. See Micah 5:2 and Luke 2:1–19.

b 2:1 Or "in the land of Judea." The Hebrew gospel of Matthew is "the land of Judah."

c 2:1 Herod died in 4 BC, which helps in dating the birth of Christ.

d 2:1 Or "astrologers," known as dream interpreters. These wealthy priests would have traveled with an entourage for protection as officials from the East. The Greek word *magos* is taken from the Mede language and means "spiritual advisors" or simply "priests." They were appointed by Darius over the state religion as priests of Persia, which is modern-day Iran, and served as official advisors to the king. By the time of Jesus' birth, Persia had been conquered and was being governed by successors to Alexander the Great. It is possible these Magos came from the Mesopotamian region of Seleucia. See also Daniel 2 and 5:11, where the prophet Daniel is given the title of "Chief of the Magio." It is probable that these Magos were descendants of those who had been taught by Daniel, and because of his prophecy of the Messiah being "cut off," they may have been able to decipher the date of his birth along with the interpretation of his star rising.

e 2:2 Or "his star in the east" or "shooting star" or possibly "comet." The Shem-Tob translation of the Hebrew Matthew accounts is plural, "stars," which fits recorded astronomical accounts of multiple stars rising from 6 BC to 2 BC. Note that it is also called "*his* star," not the star of Bethlehem.

⁵"He will be born in Bethlehem, in the land of Judah," they told him. "Because the prophecy states:

⁶And you, little Bethlehem, are not insignificant
Among the clans of Judah, for out of you will emerge
The Shepherd-King*ᵃ* **of My people Israel!"***ᵇ*

⁷Then Herod secretly summoned the spiritual priests from the East to ascertain the exact time the star first appeared. ⁸And he told them, "Now go to Bethlehem and carefully look there for the child, and when you've found him, report to me so that I can go and bow down and worship him too."

⁹And so they left, and on their way to Bethlehem, suddenly the same star they had seen in the East reappeared! Amazed, they watched as it went ahead of them and stopped directly over the place where the child was. ¹⁰And when they saw the star, they were so ecstatic that they shouted and celebrated with unrestrained joy.*ᶜ* ¹¹When they came into the house and saw the young child with Mary, his mother, they were overcome. Falling to the ground at his feet they worshipped him.*ᵈ* Then they opened their treasure boxes*ᵉ* full of gifts and presented him with gold, frankincense, and myrrh. ¹²Afterward they returned to their own country by another route because God had warned them in a dream not to go back to Herod.

---

a 2:6 As translated from the Aramaic. The Greek is "the Leader who will shepherd my people Israel."

b 2:6 See Micah 5:2. Both the Septuagint and the Shem-Tob (Hebrew Matthew) have "out of you will come to me a Ruler who will be King of Israel." The Septuagint adds, "He will shepherd my people in the strength of the Lord."

c 2:10 The Greek is hard to translate since it contains so many redundant words for joy in this one verse. It is literally, "They rejoiced with a great joy exceedingly." They were ecstatic!

d 2:11 Turning their backs on human wisdom, these "wise men" bowed low before the true Wisdom of God. See 1 Corinthians 1:24.

e 2:11 These "wise men" were extremely wealthy. They presented gifts that totaled a great sum of money—not tiny presents wrapped with bows, but treasure chests full of financial wealth. Although we are not given the monetary value of each type of gift, we know that frankincense and myrrh were extremely costly. These gifts would have financed Joseph and Mary and Jesus' exodus to Egypt and supplied their living expenses for a number of years, even after returning to Israel. Gold is an often-used symbol of the deity of Christ. Frankincense points to His perfect life of holiness, excellence, and devotion. Myrrh, an embalming spice, speaks to us of the suffering love that would lead him to the death of the cross.

They Escape to Egypt

[13]After they had gone, Joseph had another dream. An angel of the Lord appeared to him and said, "Get up now and flee to Egypt. Take Mary and the little child and stay there until I tell you to leave, for Herod intends to search for the child to kill him."

[14]So that very night he got up and took Jesus and his mother and made their escape to Egypt [15]and remained there until Herod died. All of this fulfilled what the Lord had spoken through his prophet:

I summon my Son out of Egypt.[a]

[16]When Herod realized that he had been tricked by the wise men, he was infuriated. So he sent soldiers with orders to slaughter every baby boy two years old and younger in Bethlehem and throughout the surrounding countryside, based on the time frame he was given from interrogating the wise men. [17]This fulfilled the words of the prophet Jeremiah:

[18]I hear the screams of anguish,
Weeping, and wailing in Ramah.
Rachel is weeping uncontrollably for her children.[b]
And she refuses to be comforted,
Because they are dead and gone.[c]

They Return to Nazareth

[19]After Herod died, the angel of the Lord appeared again to Joseph in a dream while he was still in Egypt, [20]saying, "Go back to the land of Israel and take the child and his mother with you, for those who sought to kill the child are dead."

[21]So he awoke and took Jesus and Mary and returned to the land of

---

a 2:15 See Hosea 11:1. Both Jesus and the nation of Israel came up out of Egypt.
b 2:18 As translated from the Septuagint. *Rachel* becomes a metaphor for all of Israel.
c 2:18 See Jeremiah 31:14–15.

Israel. [22]But when he heard that Archelaus, Herod's son, had succeeded him as ruler over all of the territory of Judah, he was afraid to go back. Then he had another dream from God, warning him to avoid that region and instructing him instead to go to the province of Galilee. [23]So he settled his family in the village of Nazareth, fulfilling the prophecy that he would be known as the "Branch."[a]

---

a 2:23 Or "a Nazarene." The Hebrew Scriptures give us a wonderful truth about the Branch (Sprout) of the Lord that would come and establish righteousness. The word for "branch" or sprout is *netzer*, the root word from which Nazareth, Nazarene, and Nazarite come. The teaching of the Branch of the Lord is a concept taught throughout the Bible, from the Tree of Life, to the seven branches of the Lampstand, to Jesus the Vine calling us his branches. Jesus is a Scion, a Branch that can be transplanted and grafted into a human life. Another variant form of this amazing word *netzer* can be translated "keeper, watchman, one who keeps secrets, guardian, one who keeps watch." All of these words are true of Jesus, the Branch who was raised in the village of the Branch (Nazareth). Additionally, the Aramaic word for Nazareth means "heir of a powerful family" or "victorious one." So it is entirely possible to translate this "He will be called the Victorious Branch (of Nazareth)." See Daniel 11:7, Isaiah 4:2, Isaiah 11:1 and 60:21. See also Isaiah 4:2, Jeremiah 23:5, and Zechariah 6:12, which uses a Hebrew synonym for Branch, *tsemach*.

$\mathcal{T}hree$

___

John the Baptizer

[1]It was at this time that John the Baptizer[a] began to preach in the desert of Judah.[b] His message was this: [2]"The reign of heaven's kingdom[c] is about to appear—so you'd better keep turning away from evil and turn back to God!"[d]

[3]Isaiah was referring to John when he prophesied:

A thunderous voice! One will be crying out in the wilderness
"Prepare yourself for the Lord's coming
And level a straight path inside your hearts for him."[e]

[4]Now, John wore clothing made from camel's hair, tied at his waist with a leather strap, and his food consisted of dried locusts[f] and wild honey. [5]A steady stream of people from Jerusalem, all the surrounding countryside,[g] and the region near the Jordan came out to the wilderness to be baptized by him. [6]And while they were publicly confessing their sins, he would immerse them in the Jordan River.

---

a 3:1 Or "John the Immerser." The name John means "Yahweh has graced him."
b 3:1 This was the desert region west of the Dead Sea including the lower Jordan. The prophet John was of a priestly family and possibly a member of the Qumran community of the Essenes.
c 3:2 Or "the kingdom realm of heaven." The word *heaven* is found 238 times in the New Testament and *hell* 23 times.
d 3:2 Or "repent." John was preaching in Aramaic, the language of the day. The word for "repent" in both Hebrew and Aramaic means "to return to God (and leave your sins behind)." This is much more than simply changing your mind; it is a powerful term for turning your life around and coming back to the holy God.
e 3:3 See Isaiah 40:3, which is quoted in all four gospels. The Aramaic has in place of Lord, "Lord Yahweh," an obvious implication of the deity of Christ. Isaiah's prophecy is more than a road-construction project. He uses the metaphor of clearing a path as a parable of cleansing our hearts and being prepared in our hearts to receive the Christ.
f 3:4 See Leviticus 11:22, Joel 1:4, 2 Kings 1:8, Zechariah 13:4, Malachi 4:5–6, and Matthew 11:14.
g 3:5 Or "Judea."

⁷But when he saw many coming from among the wealthy elite of Jewish society[a] and many of the religious leaders known as "separated ones"[b] coming to witness the baptism, he began to denounce them, saying, "You offspring of vipers! Who warned you to slither away like snakes from the fire of God's judgment?[c] ⁸You must prove your repentance by a changed life. ⁹And don't presume you can get away with merely saying to yourselves, 'But we're Abraham's descendants!' For I tell you, God can awaken these stones to become sons of Abraham![d] ¹⁰The axe[e] is now ready to cut down the trees at their very roots. Every fruitless, rotten tree will be chopped down and thrown into the fire. ¹¹Those who repent I baptize with water, but there is coming a Man after me who is more powerful than I am. In fact, I'm not even worthy enough to pick up his sandals. He will submerge you into union with the Spirit of Holiness and with a raging fire![f] ¹²He comes with a winnowing fork[g] in his hands and comes to his threshing floor to sift what is worthless from what is pure. And he is ready to sweep out his threshing floor and gather his wheat into his granary,[h] but the straw he will burn up with a fire that can't be extinguished!"

¹³Then Jesus left Galilee to come to the Jordan to be baptized by John. ¹⁴But when he waded into the water, John resisted him, saying, "Why are you doing this? I'm the one who needs to be baptized by you, and yet you come to be baptized by me?"

a 3:7 Or "the Sadducees."
b 3:7 Or "Pharisees." The Pharisees and Sadducees were two of the sects of Judaism of that day.
c 3:7 Implied in the text. John is telling them they can't escape the fire of judgment just by getting wet.
d 3:9 There is an interesting word-play in the Hebrew and Aramaic that is lost in an English translation. The Hebrew word for sons (běnayyā) and stones ('abnayyā) are similar. God builds His house with sons, not stones. John baptized the people at the place of the crossing of the Jordan during the time of Joshua. After their miracle crossing of the Jordan they were instructed to set up twelve stones, representing the twelve sons of Israel, as a memorial. Perhaps John the Baptizer was referencing those very stones from which God could raise up as sons.
e 3:10 The axe becomes a metaphor of the word of truth that judges hearts and nations.
f 3:11 The text is somewhat ambiguous as to what fire is spoken of. Some see it as the fire of judgment, yet Jesus sent us the Holy Spirit, who baptized his church in fire at Pentecost. This last clause is a hendiadys and could be translated "He will baptize you in the raging fire of the Holy Spirit!"
g 3:12 This winnowing fork was like a pitchfork that would thresh grain by throwing it into the air so the wind could blow away the chaff.
h 3:12 See Isaiah 41:15–16.

[15]Jesus replied, **"It is only right to do all that God requires."**[a] Then John baptized Jesus.[b] [16]And as[c] Jesus rose up out of the water, the heavenly realm opened up over him[d] and he saw the Holy Spirit descend out of the heavens and rest upon him in the form of a dove.[e] [17]Then suddenly the voice of the Father shouted from the sky, saying, **"This is the Son I love, and my greatest delight is in him."**[f]

---

a 3:15 Or "fulfill all righteousness (complete every righteous requirement)." This was the presentation of the Lamb of God as the sacrifice for sins. It was important that John publicly wash the Lamb of God and fulfill the requirements of the law, proving to Israel that the Lamb that was soon to be offered was spotless and without blemish. There are four baptisms in this chapter: 1) John baptizing with water, 2) Father God baptizing Jesus with the power of heaven, 3) Jesus will baptize believers with the same Holy Spirit, 4) the baptism of fire.

b 3:15 Jesus would have been about thirty years old, the age when Levitical priests were ordained and qualified to serve. This was his ordination as the High Priest over the household of faith. Jesus' baptism was a form of dedication. Like Solomon, who dedicated the temple, John now dedicates the temple of Jesus' body, the dwelling place of God. In a sense, John was the true high priest who was ordaining his replacement. Jesus was not repenting, but offering himself as God's sinless Lamb.

c 3:16 There are Latin manuscripts and external evidence dating to Jerome indicating that the Hebrew Matthew included this sentence: "A great light flashed from the water, so that all who had gathered there were afraid." (Diatessaron and Romanos Melodos, *First Hymn on the Epiphany*, XVI.14.7–10.)

d 3:16 See also Acts 7:56.

e 3:16 The dove is a symbol for both meekness and purity. Two gentle animals are pictured at the baptism of Jesus, a dove resting upon a lamb. If you want the presence of the Dove you need to have the nature of the Lamb. The implication is that the Holy Spirit came upon Jesus and never left him.

f 3:17 Or "In him I find my delight." See also Isaiah 42:1 and Psalm 2:7. The church historian Jerome affirms that additional words were spoken by the Father: "My Son, in all the prophets I was waiting for you, that you might come and I might rest in you. For you are my rest and my firstborn Son, who reigns forever!" (*The Gospel of Matthew for the Hebrews* and *Commentary on Isaiah Chapter 4*. Throckmorton: 14 fn. Nicholson: 43. OMG II: 156 *et seq.*)

Four
___

Jesus Tempted by the Devil

[1]Afterward, the Holy Spirit led Jesus into the lonely wilderness in order to reveal his strength against the accuser[a] by going through the ordeal of testing.[b] [2]And after fasting for forty days,[c] Jesus was extremely weak and famished. [3]Then the tempter came to entice him to provide food by doing a miracle. So he said to Jesus, "How can you possibly be the Son of God and go hungry? Just order these stones to be turned into loaves of bread."

[4]He answered, **"The Scriptures say:**

> **Bread alone will not satisfy,[d]**
> **But true life is found in every word**
> **Which constantly goes forth from God's mouth."[e]**

[5]Then the accuser transported Jesus to the holy city of Jerusalem and perched him at the highest point[f] of the temple [6]and said to him, "If you're

---

a 4:1 Or "devil." The Aramaic word for "devil" means "accuser." The Greek word is "slanderer."
b 4:1 Or "tribulation." God also tested Israel for forty years in the wilderness. See Deuteronomy 8:2.
c 4:2 Moses and Elijah both fasted forty days. See Exodus 34:28 and 1 Kings 19:8. The number forty usually signifies passing a test or enduring a time of trial. It rained for forty days in the time of Noah, and Jonah warned Nineveh for forty days. God told Ezekiel to lay on his right side for forty days (Ezekiel 4:6).
d 4:4 Or "Man will not live by bread alone." The Aramaic is "Bar-nasha" and can be translated "The Son of Man will not live by bread alone."
e 4:4 See Deuteronomy 8:3. God had not given Jesus permission to turn stones into bread, and Jesus would not be pushed into prematurely demonstrating his power. He was content with the timing of his Father. He refused to turn stones into bread to feed himself, but he multiplied bread for his hungry followers. Today he is still turning hearts of stone into living bread that will feed the nations with truth.
f 4:5 Or "wing." See Psalm 91:4.

really God's Son, jump, and the angels will catch you. For it is written in the Scriptures:

> He will command His angels to protect you
> And they will lift you up
> So that you won't even bruise your foot on a rock.[a]

[7]Once again Jesus said to him, **"The Scriptures say:**

> **You must never put the Lord your God to a test."**[b]

[8]And the third time the accuser lifted Jesus up into a very high mountain range and showed him all the kingdoms of the world and all the splendor that goes with it.

[9]"All of these kingdoms I will give to you," the accuser said, "if only you will kneel down before me and worship me."

[10]But Jesus said, **"Go away, enemy![c] For the Scriptures say:**

> **Kneel before the Lord your God**
> **And worship only him."**[d]

[11]At once the accuser left him, and angels suddenly gathered around Jesus to minister to his needs.

Jesus Preaches in Galilee

[12]When Jesus heard that John the Baptizer had been thrown into prison, he went back into Galilee. [13]Jesus moved from Nazareth to make his home in

---

a 4:6 See Psalm 91:11–12 and Matthew 26:53. This was a temptation to capitalize on being the Son of God and force God to protect him as he jumped. Jesus was being tested over restraining his power as the Anointed One and waiting until the timing of his Father in publicly releasing him to work miracles and display his power. He was not sent to throw himself down from the temple, but to throw down the temple and establish a new order of worship, as a true relationship with God is internal with every believer now becoming the temple of God. See 1 Corinthians 3:16 and 6:19.

b 4:7 See Deuteronomy 6:16.

c 4:10 Or "Satan."

d 4:10 See Deuteronomy 6:13–14.

Capernaum,[a] which is by Lake Galilee in the land of Zebulun and Naphtali. [14]He did this to make the prophecy of Isaiah come true:

> [15]**Listen, you who live in the land of Zebulun**
> **And the land of Naphtali,**
> **Along the road to the sea**
> **And on the other side of the Jordan,**
> **And Galilee—the land of non-Jewish peoples!**
> [16]**You who spend your days shrouded in darkness**
> **Can now say, "We have seen a brilliant Light."[b]**
> **And those who live in the dark shadow land of death**
> **Can now say, "The Dawning Light arises on us."**

[17]From that time on Jesus began to proclaim his message with these words: **"Keep turning away from your sins and come back to God, for heaven's reigning kingdom is now accessible."[c]**

Jesus Calls His Disciples

[18]As he was walking by the shore of Lake Galilee, Jesus noticed two fishermen who were brothers. One was nicknamed Keefa[d] (later called Peter), and the other was Andrew, his brother. Watching as they were casting their nets into the water, [19]Jesus called out to them and said, **"Come and follow me, and I will transform you into men who catch people for God."[e]** [20]Immediately they dropped their nets and left everything behind to follow Jesus.

---

a 4:13 Capernaum means "the village of Nahum." It was a fishing village on the northwestern shore of the Lake of Galilee. Nahum means "pleasant."

b 4:16 Light is a common name for the Messiah in rabbinical literature. It speaks of both Christ and the revelation teaching he brings. See Isaiah 9:1–2. The Aramaic word for Galilee (*Galeela*) means "revelation of God." Jesus was raised and ministered in the land of the "revelation of God."

c 4:17 Or "heaven's kingdom realm is close enough to touch!"

d 4:18 Or "Simon." The Aramaic is Keefa, which means "the rock" or "pebble." Peter (Petros) is his Greek name.

e 4:19 Or "fishers of men." The Aramaic word can be either "fishers" or "hunters." See Ezekiel 47:1–10.

²¹Leaving there, Jesus found three other men sitting in a boat, mending their nets. Two were brothers, James and John, and they were with their father, Zebedee.ᶠ Jesus called James and John to his side and said to them, **"Come and follow Me."ᵍ** ²²And at once they left their boat and their father, and began to follow Jesus.

Jesus' Ministry of Healing

²³Jesus ministered from place to place throughout all of the province of Galilee. He taughtʰ in the Jewish meeting houses,ⁱ preaching the hope of the kingdom realmʲ and healing every kind of sickness and disease among the people. ²⁴His fame spread everywhere!ᵏ Many people who were in pain and suffering with every kind of illness were brought to Jesus for their healing—epileptics,ˡ paralytics, and those tormented by demonic powers were all set free. Everyone who was brought to Jesus was healed!

²⁵This resulted in massive crowds of people following him, including people from Galilee, Jerusalem, the land of Judah, the region of the Ten Cities known as the Decapolis, and beyond the Jordan River.ᵐ

---

f 4:21 Zebedee's name means "my gift." The gift he gave to Jesus was his two sons. All parents have the privilege of giving their children back to God.

g 4:21 Implied in the text.

h 4:23 The Greek word *didasko* is a word often used for providing skilled training.

i 4:23 Or "in their synagogues."

j 4:23 As translated from the Aramaic. The Hebrew Matthew is "the good gift of the kingdom of the heavens." The Greek is "the good news of heaven's reign."

k 4:24 As translated from the Hebrew Matthew. The Greek is "into Syria."

l 4:24 Or "the mentally ill."

m 4:25 This was the first encounter the non-Jewish peoples of the Middle East had with Jesus. He was proclaiming his universal kingdom and inviting all to enter into it.

$$Five$$

Jesus' Sermon on the Hillside

¹One day Jesus saw a vast crowd of people gathering to hear him, so he went up the slope of a hill and sat down. With his followers and disciples spread over the hillside, ²Jesus began to teach them:[a]

³**"What wealth is offered to you**[b] **when you feel your spiritual poverty!**[c] **For there is no charge to enter the realm of heaven's kingdom.**

⁴**"What delight comes to you when you wait upon the Lord!**[d] **For you will find what you long for.**[e]

---

a 5:2 It should be noted that Matthew 5–7, commonly known as the Sermon on the Mount, is the Messianic Torah and the Constitution of the kingdom of heaven. Jesus begins with giving his followers a superior way to live than the Ten Commandments of Moses. It is a superior version of all that God expects and provides for those who yield to him. Jesus gives us more than laws; he gives us promises of power to fulfill all that he asks of us. The emphasis is not on outward duty but on the inward transformation of our hearts by grace. God's kingdom is offered to those who will learn the ways of Christ and offer themselves to him in full surrender.

b 5:3 Or, "Blessed are they." The Aramaic word *toowayhon* means "enriched, happy, fortunate, delighted, blissful, content, blessed." Our English word *blessed* can indeed fit here, but *toowayhon* implies great happiness, prosperity, abundant goodness, and delight! The word *bliss* captures all of this meaning. *Toowayhon* means to have the capacity to enjoy union and communion with God. Because the meaning of the word goes beyond merely being "blessed," the translation uses different phrases for each of the Beatitudes. Verses 3–10 are presented with third-person pronouns; however, it is not abstract truth, but spoken directly to Jesus' disciples. This is why the translation is in the second person. The implication of this verse is that the poor in spirit have only one remedy, and that is trusting in God. This total reliance upon God is the doorway into the kingdom realm. Notice the obvious parallel between Isaiah 61:1–2 and these "beatitudes."

c 5:3 Or, "humble in spirit," or, "poor in spirit," which means to be humble and totally dependent upon God for everything. It is synonymous with "pious" or "saintly," not just in the sense of those who possess nothing. It could be translated "Delighted are those who have surrendered completely to God and trust only in him." See also Isaiah 41:17, 57:15, and 66:2.

d 5:4 As translated from the Hebrew Matthew. (See also Psalm 27:14.) The Greek is "mourn (grieve)." The Hebrew word for "wait" and for "mourn" is almost identical.

e 5:4 As translated from the Aramaic word for comfort, *nethbayoon*, which means "to see the face of what (or who) you long for." The Greek is "They shall be comforted."

⁵"What contentment floods you when gentleness[a] lives in you! For you will inherit the earth.[b]

⁶"How enriched you are when you crave righteousness![c] For you will be surrounded with fruitfulness.[d]

⁷"How satisfied you are when you demonstrate tender mercy![e] For tender mercy will be demonstrated to you.

⁸"What bliss you experience when your heart is pure![f] For then your eyes will open to see more and more of God.[g]

⁹"How blessed you are when you make peace! For then you will be recognized as a true child of God.[h]

¹⁰"How enriched you are when you bear the wounds of being persecuted[i] for doing what is right![j] For that is when you experience the realm of heaven's kingdom.

¹¹"How ecstatic you can be when people insult[k] and persecute you and speak all kinds of cruel lies about you because of your love for me![l] ¹²So leap for joy—since your heavenly reward is great. For you are being rejected the same way the prophets were before you.

---

a 5:5 Or "meekness." Jesus is saying that when you claim nothing as yours, everything will be given to you. The Aramaic word, *makeekheh*, implies being both gentle and flexible.

b 5:5 See Psalm 37:11 and 149:4.

c 5:6 Or "goodness" or "justice."

d 5:6 As translated from the Aramaic word *nesbhoon*, which is associated with planting and fruitfulness. The Greek is "They shall be satisfied." See Zephaniah 2:3 and Psalm 11:3–7.

e 5:7 Or "merciful to forgive." The Hebraic and Aramaic concept of mercy is that it comes from our innermost being. The root word for "mercy" is the root word for "womb." See Psalm 18:25, Proverbs 14:21, 2 Samuel 22:26, and James 2:13.

f 5:8 Or "when your heart is full of innocence." See Psalm 15:1–2, 24:4, and 51:10.

g 5:8 The Aramaic word used for "see" is *nahzon* and can be translated either in the present tense ("They see God") or the future tense ("They will see God"). The Greek is "They will progressively see God." See also Psalm 17:15.

h 5:9 See Psalm 72:3-7, Psalm 122:8–9, and Isaiah 26:12.

i 5:10 The Aramaic is "being rejected."

j 5:10 See Psalm 38:20, Isaiah 66:5, 1 Peter 3:14, and Acts 5:41. The Hebrew Matthew is "for the Righteous One."

k 5:11 The Aramaic is "criticize you" (Peter 3:14; Acts 5:41). The Hebrew Matthew is "for the Righteous One."

l 5:11 See Psalm 119:85–87. We are to live in such a way that people have to lie when they speak evil of a believer in Christ.

¹³"Your lives are like salt among the people. But if you, like salt, become bland, how can your 'saltiness' be restored? Flavorless salt is good for nothing[a] and will be thrown out and trampled on by others.

¹⁴"Your lives light up the world. Let others see your light from a distance, for how can you hide a city that stands on a hilltop?[b] ¹⁵And who would light a lamp and then hide it in an obscure place?[c] Instead, it's placed where everyone in the house can benefit from its light. ¹⁶So don't hide your light![d] Let it shine brightly before others, so that the commendable things you do will shine as light upon them, and then they will give their praise to your Father in heaven."

Fulfillment of the Law

¹⁷"If you think I've come to set aside the Law of Moses or the writings of the prophets, you're mistaken. I have come to fulfill and bring to perfection all that has been written. ¹⁸Indeed, I assure you, as long as heaven and earth endure, not even the smallest detail[e] of the Law will be done away with until its purpose is complete.[f] ¹⁹So whoever violates[g] even the least important of the commandments,[h] and teaches others to do so, will be the least esteemed in the realm of heaven's kingdom. But whoever obeys them and teaches their truths to others will be greatly esteemed in the

a 5:13 Or "Salt that has lost its flavor is *foolish*." Both Greek and Aramaic use a word that can mean either "good for nothing" or "foolish." If salt that has lost its flavor is foolish, then salt that keeps its flavor is wise. Rabbinical literature equates salt with wisdom. After speaking of salt, Jesus speaks of lighting a lamp. It was a common practice in the time of Jesus to put salt on the wick of a lamp to increase its brightness. The "salt" of wisdom will make our lights shine even brighter. Eduard Schweizer, *The Good News According to Matthew* (Atlanta: John Knox Press, 1975). W. A. Elwell and P. W. Comfort, *Tyndale Bible Dictionary* (Wheaton, Ill.: Tyndale House, Tyndale reference library, 2001), Lamp, Lampstand. 797–8.

b 5:14 See Isaiah 49:6.

c 5:15 Or "under a basket."

d 5:16 The Aramaic word for "light" (*noohra*) is often used as a metaphor for teachings that bring enlightenment and revelation into the hearts of men. Light can also represent the presence of God ("the light of his countenance"). Jesus is the light of God within us.

e 5:18 Or "not even one letter or even a part of the letter of the law."

f 5:18 Or "All its teachings come true."

g 5:19 Or "whoever loosens (diminishes)."

h 5:19 Or "these implanted goals."

realm of heaven's kingdom. [20]For I tell you, unless your lives are more pure and full of integrity[a] than the religious scholars[b] and the "separated ones," you will never experience the realm of heaven's kingdom."

Anger

[21]"You're familiar with the commandment that the older generation was taught, 'Do not murder or you will be judged.'[c] [22]But I'm telling you, if you hold anger in your heart[d] toward a fellow believer, you are subject to judgment.[e] And whoever demeans and insults[f] a fellow believer is answerable to the congregation.[g] And whoever calls down curses upon a fellow believer[h] is in danger of being sent to a fiery hell.[i]

[23]"So then, if you are presenting a gift before the altar in the temple and suddenly you remember a quarrel you have with a fellow believer, [24]leave your gift there in front of the altar and go at once to apologize with the one who is offended. Then, after you have reconciled,[j] come to the altar and present your gift. [25]It is always better to come to terms with the one who wants to sue you before you go to trial, or you may be found guilty by the judge, and he will hand you over to the officers, who will throw you into prison. [26]Believe me, you won't get out of prison until you have paid the full amount!"

---

a 5:20 Or "your deeds of righteousness."

b 5:20 Or "scribes," who were considered to be the expert theologians of the Scriptures.

c 5:21 See Exodus 20:13 and Deuteronomy 5:17.

d 5:22 Some manuscripts add, "without a cause." See 1 John 3:15. Both Aramaic and Hebrew Matthew read, "if you provoke a fellow believer to anger," or, "if you cause offense to the spirit of your brother."

e 5:22 The implication is that you would be judged as a murderer. Anger and murder are equally odious in God's eyes. Angry words kill.

f 5:22 The Aramaic is *raca* and can mean "spittle" or "lunatic." It is a word that could imply calling a fellow believer demon-possessed. The Greek is "worthless fool, imbecile."

g 5:22 Or "council (Sanhedrin)."

h 5:22 Or "whoever calls him a worthless fool." It is a word that could imply calling a fellow believer demon-possessed.

i 5:22 Or "the Gehenna of fire." Gehenna, which was an actual place where garbage was burned outside of Jerusalem, became a figure of speech for hell in the days of Jesus. It used to be the site of child sacrifice to the god Molech. See 2 Chronicles 33:6.

j 5:24 A true heart of repentance means attempting to heal severed relationships, not just empty words.

Adultery

[27]"Your ancestors have been taught, 'Never commit adultery.'[a] [28]However, I say to you, if you look with lust in your eyes at the body of a woman who is not your wife, you've already committed adultery in your heart.[b] [29]If your right eye seduces you to fall into sin,[c] then go blind in your right eye![d] For you're better off losing sight in one eye than to have your whole body thrown into hell. [30]And if your right hand entices you to sin, let it go limp and useless![e] For you're better off losing a part of your body than to have it all thrown into hell.[f]

[31]"It has been said, 'Whoever divorces his wife must give her legal divorce papers.'[g] [32]However, I say to you, if anyone divorces his wife for any reason, except for infidelity, causes her to commit adultery, and whoever marries a divorced[h] woman commits adultery."

Making Oaths

[33]"Again, your ancestors were taught, 'Never swear an oath that you don't intend to keep,[i] but keep your vows to the Lord God.'[j] [34]However, I say to you, don't bind yourself by taking an oath at all. Don't swear by heaven,

---

a 5:27 See Exodus 20:14.
b 5:28 The Aramaic is speaking of more than adultery with a married woman; it uses the word for any sex act outside of marriage. Jesus elevates the standard of righteousness. He is holy, and when he comes to live within the believer, his holiness is the fulfillment of what God requires of us.
c 5:29 The Greek word *skandalizo* means to "entice to sin," "offend," or "set a trap."
d 5:29 Or "Pluck out your eye and throw it away."
e 5:30 Or "Cut it off and throw it away." Verses 29 and 30 use obvious hyperbole to help us understand how intent we must be to guard our lives from sin.
f 5:30 Jesus is using an obvious figure of speech when he instructs us to "pluck out" our eyes or "cut off" our hands. The metaphor is clear: we are to end every evil habit that will lead us to destruction.
g 5:31 See Deuteronomy 24:1. By serving her divorce papers, a husband was required to return his wife's dowry. The divorced woman would then leave his house and receive back her dowry.
h 5:32 The Aramaic can be translated "whoever marries a woman who is separated and not divorced."
i 5:33 That is, don't perjure yourself.
j 5:33 See Leviticus 19:12 and Isaiah 66:1.

for heaven is where God's throne is placed.[a] [35]Don't swear an oath by the earth, because it is the rug under God's feet,[b] and not by Jerusalem, because it is the city of the Great King.[c] [36]And why would you swear by your own head, because it's not in your power to turn a single hair white or black? But just let your words ring true.[d] [37]A simple 'Yes' or 'No' will suffice. Anything beyond this springs from a deceiver.[e]

[38]"Your ancestors have also been taught, 'Take an eye in exchange for an eye and a tooth in exchange for a tooth.'[f] [39]However, I say to you, don't repay an evil act with another evil act.[g] But whoever insults you by slapping you on the right cheek, turn the other to him as well.[h] [40]If someone is determined to sue you for your coat, give him the shirt off your back as a gift in return. [41]And should people in authority take advantage of you, do more than what they demand.[i] [42]Learn to generously share what you have with those who ask for help, and don't close your heart to the one who comes to borrow from you."[j]

---

a   5:34 In the days of Jesus and in the Middle Eastern cultural setting of Israel, taking oaths and swearing by something greater than oneself was a common practice. Jesus' words trump culture and our bondage to doing things according to the expected norms of society. He instructs us to be faithful and true with our words.

b   5:35 As translated from the Aramaic. The Greek is "his footstool."

c   5:35 See Psalm 48:2.

d   5:36 A summary conclusion implied in the context. Our words must be fulfilled by actions. All four things Jesus mentioned were considered sacred to the Jewish people—heaven, earth, Jerusalem, and head. But Jesus teaches us that words of truth make our lives sacred. See James 5:12.

e   5:37 As translated from the Aramaic. The Greek is "Don't resist the evil (one)."See Ecclesiastes 5:4–7.

f   5:38 See Exodus 21:24.

g   5:39 As translated from Hebrew Matthew. The Greek is "Do not resist evil (or evil doer)."

h   5:39 That is, simply stand and take it without responding in return with violence. In the cultural setting of the days of Jesus, to slap someone was the greatest insulting physical blow you could give a person. It is better to respond with kindness. This robs the oppressor of his ability to humiliate. See Proverbs 15:1, Proverbs 24:29, Isaiah 50:6, and Lamentations 3:30.

i   5:41 "If someone forces you to go a mile with him, go two." This is in reference to the Roman authorities, who often compelled the Jewish men to carry their heavy items for them. In verse 40 we are challenged to give up our rights, in verse 41 to surrender our freedom, and in verse 42 to surrender our prosperity.

j   5:41 The Aramaic is "If someone wants to benefit from you, do not stop him." In the Agrapha sayings of Jesus, as quoted by early church fathers, an additional line is found here that reads, "It is more blessed to give than to receive." See also Acts 20:35.

Love Your Enemies

43"Your ancestors have also been taught 'Love your neighbors[a] and hate the one who hates you.' 44However, I say to you, love your enemy, bless the one who curses you, do something wonderful for the one who hates you,[b] and respond to the very ones who persecute you by praying for them. 45For that will reveal your identity as children of your heavenly Father. He is kind to all by bringing the sunrise to warm and rainfall to refresh whether a person does what is good or evil. 46What reward do you deserve if you only love the loveable? Don't even the tax collectors[c] do that? 47How are you any different from others if you limit your kindness[d] only to your friends? Don't even the ungodly[e] do that? 48Since you are children of a perfect Father in heaven, you are to be perfect like him."[f]

a 5:43 The Aramaic is "your relatives." This phrase is found in the Torah; the following phrase is from oral tradition. See Leviticus 19:18.
b 5:44 As translated from the Aramaic. The previous two clauses are not found in some reliable Greek manuscripts.
c 5:46 The Hebrew Matthew is "transgressors."
d 5:47 Or "Ask for the peace of your brothers" (Hebrew Matthew and Aramaic).
e 5:47 Or "Gentiles (who worship other gods)."
f 5:48 The Greek and Aramaic words for "perfect" can also mean "whole, complete, fully mature, lacking nothing, all-inclusive, well rounded."

Six

Giving with Pure Motives

[1]"Examine your motives to make sure you're not showing off when you do your good deeds, only to be admired by others; otherwise, you will lose the reward of your heavenly Father. [2]So when you give to the poor, don't announce it and make a show of it just to be seen by people,[a] like the hypocrites[b] in the streets and in the marketplace.[c] They've already received their reward! [3]But when you demonstrate generosity, do it with pure motives and without drawing attention to yourself.[d] [4]Give secretly and your Father, who sees all you do, will reward you openly."[e]

Prayer

[5]"Whenever you pray, be sincere and not like the pretenders who love the attention they receive while praying before others in the meetings and on street corners. Believe me, they've already received in full their reward. [6]But whenever you pray, go into your innermost chamber and be alone with Father God,[f] praying to him in secret. And your Father, who sees all you do, will reward you openly. [7]When you pray, there is no need to repeat

---

a 6:2 Or "blow your own horn."

b 6:2 The Greek word *hupokrites* is not only used for people with double standards. It actually means "overcritical, nitpicking, splitting hairs over religious issues."

c 6:2 As translated from Aramaic and Hebrew Matthew. The Greek is "synagogues."

d 6:3 Or "Don't let your left hand know what your right hand is doing." This is a figure of speech for giving with pure motives, not to be seen and applauded by others.

e 6:4 As translated from the Aramaic and Hebrew Matthew. Most Greek manuscripts do not include the word *openly*.

f 6:6 Or "Go into your inner room (storehouse), close the door, and pray." This "inner room" can also be a metaphor for praying from the heart, from our innermost being, our storehouse.

empty phrases, praying like those who don't know God,[a] for they expect God to hear them because of their many words. [8]There is no need to imitate them, since your Father already knows what you need before you ask him.[9] Pray like this:

> 'Our Father, dwelling in the heavenly realms,
> May the glory of your name
> Be the center on which our lives turn.[b]
> [10]Manifest your kingdom realm,[c]
> And cause your every purpose to be fulfilled on earth,
> Just as it is fulfilled in heaven.
> [11]We acknowledge you as our Provider
> Of all we need each day.[d]
> [12]Forgive us the wrongs we have done[e] as we ourselves
> Release forgiveness to those who have wronged us.
> [13]Rescue us every time we face tribulation[f]
> And set us free from evil.[g]
> For you are the King who rules
> With power and glory forever. Amen.'[h]

a 6:7 Or "Gentiles."

b 6:9 An alternate reading of the Aramaic text. The Aramaic word for "name" is *shema* (the Hebrew word, *shem*), a word with multiple meanings. It can also be translated "light," "sound," or "atmosphere." Placing a light, like a lantern, in an enclosed space magnifies that light. This is the meaning here of God's name being made sacred and magnified as we focus our lives on him. The Greek is "treated as holy."

c 6:10 Or "Come and begin your kingdom reign."

d 6:11 Or "Give us bread (or life) today for the coming day." Bread becomes a metaphor of our needs (physically, spiritually, and emotionally). Jesus is teaching us to acknowledge Father God as our Provider of all we need each day. Both the Greek and Hebrew Matthew can be translated "Give us this day our bread for tomorrow (or our continual bread)."

e 6:12 Or "Send away the results of our debts (shortcomings)," used as a metaphor for our sins. The Aramaic can be translated "Give us serenity as we also allow others serenity."

f 6:13 Or "Do not let us be put into the ordeal of testing." God never tempts man. See James 1:13–14.

g 6:13 Or "the evil one."

h 6:13 As translated from the Aramaic, Hebrew Matthew, and most Greek manuscripts. The Aramaic word for "forever" means "until the end of all the universes."

[14]"And when you pray,[a] make sure you forgive the faults of others so that your Father in heaven will also forgive you. [15]But if you withhold forgiveness from others, your Father withholds forgiveness from you."

Fasting

[16]"When you fast, don't look like those who pretend to be spiritual. They want everyone to know they're fasting, so they appear in public looking miserable, gloomy, and disheveled.[b] Believe me, they've already received their reward in full. [17-18]When you fast, don't let it be obvious, but instead, wash your face[c] and groom yourself and realize that your Father in the secret place is the one who is watching all that you do in secret and will continue to reward you openly."

Treasures in Heaven

[19]"Don't keep hoarding for yourselves earthly treasures that can be stolen by thieves. Material wealth eventually rusts, decays, and loses its value.[d] [20]Instead, stockpile heavenly treasures[e] for yourselves that cannot be stolen and will never rust, decay, or lose their value. [21]For your heart will always pursue what you value as your treasure.[f]

[22]"The eyes of your spirit allow revelation light[g] to enter into your being. If your heart is unclouded, the light floods in! [23]But if your eyes are focused on money,[h] the light cannot penetrate and darkness takes its

---

a 6:14 Implied in the context.
b 6:16 Or "disfigure their faces." Some of them would put saffron on their faces to make them appear a sickly yellow color, to be seen as though they had been fasting.
c 6:17-18 Or "Put oil on your head."
d 6:19 Or "where rust and moth destroy."
e 6:20 Heavenly treasures are eternal realities, such as loving others and doing good, revelation of truth, and bringing Christ's light to the lost. None of these "treasures" can be stolen or ever lose their value.
f 6:21 Or "For your thoughts (heart) will always be focused on your treasure."
g 6:22 The teachings of Jesus are the "revelation light" referred to here. Some scholars see "healthy eyes" as a Semitic figure of speech for generosity, due to the context of giving and money in the verses before and after.
h 6:23 Implied in the context. An "evil" eye can also be associated with being stingy and greedy.

place.[a] How profound will be the darkness within you[b] if the light of truth cannot enter!

²⁴"How could you worship two gods at the same time? You will have to hate one and love the other, or be devoted to one and despise the other. You can't worship the true God and the god of money!"[c]

Don't Worry

²⁵"This is why I tell you to never be worried about your life, for all that you need will be provided, such as food, water, clothing—everything your body needs. Isn't there more to your life than a meal? Isn't your body more than clothing?

²⁶"Look at all the birds—do you think they worry about their existence? They don't plant or reap or store up food, yet your heavenly Father provides them each with food. Aren't you much more valuable to your Father than they? ²⁷So, which one of you by worrying could add anything to your life?[d]

²⁸"And why would you worry about your clothing? Look at all the beautiful flowers of the field. They don't work or toil, ²⁹and yet not even Solomon in all his splendor was robed in beauty more than one of these! ³⁰So if God has clothed the meadow with hay, which is here for such a short time and then dried up and burned, won't he provide for you the clothes you need—even though you live with such little faith?

³¹"So then, forsake your worries! Why would you say, 'What will we eat?' or 'What will we drink?' or 'What will we wear?' ³²For that is what the

---

a 6:23 Or "If your eye is healthy (focused), your whole body is full of light; but if it is sick (evil), your body is full of darkness." The "eye" becomes a metaphor for spiritual perception. The "body" is our spirit. The "lamp" is Jesus' teachings. The "darkness" is formed by the lies and opinions that blind us. These obvious metaphors have been made explicit in the translation.

b 6:23 Hebrew Matthew is "All your ways are dark."

c 6:24 Or "God and Mammon." Mammon is an Aramaic term for money. See 1 Timothy 6:6–10. There is found after verse 24 a part of the Agrapha that reads, "If you do not fast from the world, you will never discover the kingdom of God" (Oxyrhyncus Papyrus 655, pOxy 1:4–11).

d 6:27 The Aramaic and Hebrew Matthew is "add a cubit to your height." The Greek is "add one hour to your lifespan."

unbelievers chase after. Doesn't your heavenly Father already know the things your bodies require?[a]

[33]"So above all, constantly chase after the realm of God's kingdom[b] and the righteousness that proceeds from him. Then all these less important things will be given to you abundantly.[c] [34]Refuse to worry about tomorrow, but deal with each challenge that comes your way, one day at a time.[d] Tomorrow will take care of itself."

a 6:32 There is a part of the Agrapha inserted here, which is confirmed by a number of church fathers who had access to more ancient manuscripts, which reads, "So if you ask for the great things, God will add to you the little things." This is most likely from a variation of the Hebrew Matthew. (Clement of Alexandria, *Stromateis* 1.24.158, Origen, *Commentary on the Psalms* 4.4; *De Oratione* 2.2; 14.1; Eusebius *Commentary on the Psalms* 16.2. See also Craig A. Evans, *Fabricating Jesus: How Modern Scholars Distort the Gospels* (IVP Press, 2006), 236–238.

b 6:33 The Hebrew Matthew is "Above all, pray for the kingdom realm of God."

c 6:33 As translated from the Aramaic.

d 6:34 Or "One day's trouble is enough for one day."

$$\mathscr{Seven}$$

Do Not Judge

[1]"Refuse to be a critic full of bias toward others, and judgment[a] will not be passed on you. [2]For you'll be judged by the same standard that you've used to judge others. The measurement you use on them will be used on you.[b] [3]Why would you focus on the flaw in someone else's life and yet fail to notice the glaring flaws of your own?[c] [4]How could you say to your friend, 'Let me show you where you're wrong,' when you're guilty of even more? [5]You're being hypercritical and a hypocrite![d] First acknowledge your own 'blind spots' and deal with them, and then you'll be capable of dealing with the 'blind spot' of your friend.

[6]"Who would hang earrings on a dog's ear[e] or throw pearls in front of wild pigs? They'll only trample them under their feet and then turn around and tear you to pieces!

[7]"Ask, and the gift is yours. Seek, and you'll discover. Knock, and the door will be opened for you. [8]For every persistent one will get what he asks

---

a 7:1 It is God's judgment that is being implied by the passive verbs.

b 7:2 See Romans 2:1.

c 7:3 Or "Why do you see a speck in your brother's eye but fail to see the beam of wood sticking out of your own eye?"

d 7:4 Or "You hypocrite, why don't you first remove the beam sticking out of your own eye? Then you can see clearly to remove the small speck out of your brother's eye." Jesus is clearly teaching that our blind spots prevent us from accurately evaluating the needs of others.

e 7:6 As translated from the Aramaic. The Greek is "Don't let the dogs have consecrated (holy) meat." The Aramaic word for "earrings" is almost identical to the word for "holy." Earrings and pearls are symbols of spiritual truths given to us by God. They give us beautiful "ears" to hear his voice and impart lovely pearls of wisdom, which are not to be regarded lightly or shared with those who have their hearts closed. The Aramaic word for "throw" is almost identical to the word for "to instruct" or "to teach." The value of wisdom is not appreciated by those who have no ears to hear it.

for. Every persistent seeker will discover what he longs for. And everyone who knocks persistently will one day find an open door.[a]

⁹"Do you know of any parent who would give his hungry child, who asked for food, a plate of rocks instead? ¹⁰Or when asked for a piece of fish, what parent would offer his child a snake instead? ¹¹If you, imperfect as you are,[b] know how to lovingly take care of your children and give them what's best, how much more ready is your heavenly Father to give wonderful gifts[c] to those who ask him?"

The Golden Rule

¹²"In everything you do, be careful to treat others in the same way you'd want them to treat you, for that is the essence of all the teachings of the law and the prophets."

The Narrow Gate

¹³"Come to God through the narrow gate, because the wide gate and broad path is the way that leads to destruction—nearly everyone chooses that crowded road! ¹⁴The narrow gate and the difficult way leads to eternal life—so few even find it!"

False Prophets

¹⁵"Constantly be on your guard against phony prophets. They come disguised as lambs, appearing to be genuine, but on the inside they are like wild, ravenous wolves![d] ¹⁶You can spot them by their actions, for the fruits

---

a 7:8 Clement of Alexandria attributes an additional saying to Jesus and states that it is from the Hebrew Matthew: "The one who seeks should not cease until he finds, and in finding he shall marvel, and having marveled he shall reign, and having reigned he shall rest." *Miscellanies* 2.9 (de Santos 3; Lagrange 9) and *Miscellanies* 5.14 (de Santos 4; Lagrange 10).

b 7:11 Or "although you are evil."

c 7:11 Hebrew Matthew is "give His good Spirit," a reference to asking for the Holy Spirit. See also Luke 11:13.

d 7:15 Hebrew Matthew adds a phrase, "They are full of deceit as wild, ravenous wolves." There is at least a hint here of the Benjamite prophecy found in Genesis 49:27.

of their character will be obvious. You won't find sweet grapes hanging on a thorn bush, and you'll never pick good fruit from a tumbleweed. ¹⁷⁻¹⁹So if the tree is good, it will produce good fruit; but if the tree is bad, it will bear only rotten fruit and it deserves to be cut down and burned. ²⁰Look at the obvious fruit of their lives and ministries, and then you'll know whether they are true or false."[a]

Jesus Warns of Pretenders

²¹"Not everyone who says to me, 'Lord, Lord,' will enter into the realm of heaven's kingdom. It is only those who persist in doing the will of my heavenly Father. ²²On the day of judgment many will say to me, "Lord, Lord, don't you remember us? Didn't we prophesy[b] in your name? Didn't we cast out demons and do many miracles for the sake of your name?' ²³But I will have to say to them, 'Go away from me, you lawless rebels! I've never been joined to you!'[c]

²⁴"Everyone who hears my teaching and applies it to his life can be compared to a wise man who built his house on an unshakable foundation. ²⁵When the rains fell and the flood[d] came, with fierce winds beating upon his house, it stood firm because of its strong foundation.

²⁶"But everyone who hears my teaching and does not apply it to his life can be compared to a foolish man who built his house on sand. ²⁷When it rained and rained and the flood came, with wind and waves beating upon his house, it collapsed and was swept away."[e]

a 7:20 This summary statement is implied in the text and necessary for the English narrative.
b 7:22 Or "preach in your name."
c 7:23 The Aramaic can be translated "From everlasting I have not known you."
d 7:25 Or "rivers." See also Song of Songs 8:7.
e 7:27 Or "and great was its fall!"

²⁸By the time Jesus finished speaking, the crowds were dazed and overwhelmed[a] by his teaching, ²⁹because his words carried such great authority, quite unlike their religious scholars.[b]

a 7:28 The Greek word used here, *ekplesso,* is a strong verb that means "awestruck, filled with amazement, astonished, panic stricken, something that takes your breath away (being hit with a blow), to be shocked, to expel, to drive out." Clearly, Jesus spoke with such glory and power emanating from him that his words were like thunderbolts in their hearts. May we hear his words in the same way today.
b 7:29 Or "scribes (experts of the Law)." Jesus taught from an inner knowledge of God and his Word, for his teaching emphasized obedience to God from the heart, not just outwardly keeping laws.

Eight

Jesus Heals a Leper

¹After he came down from teaching on the hillside, massive crowds began following him.[a] ²Suddenly, a leper walked up to Jesus and threw himself down before him in worship[b] and said, "Lord, you have the power to heal me...if you really want to."

³Jesus reached out his hand and touched the leper and said, **"Of course I want to heal you—be healed!"** And instantly, all signs of leprosy[c] disappeared! ⁴Then Jesus said to him, **"Don't speak to anyone, but go at once and find a priest and show him what has happened to you. Make sure to take the offering Moses commanded so they can certify your healing."**[d]

Jesus Heals the Son of a Roman Officer

⁵When Jesus entered the village of Capernaum, a captain in the Roman army[e] approached him, asking for a miracle.[f] ⁶"Lord," he said, "I have a son[g] who is lying in my home, paralyzed and suffering terribly."

⁷Jesus responded, **"I will go with you and heal him."**

⁸⁻⁹But the Roman officer interjected, "Lord, who am I to have you come into my house? I understand your authority,[h] for I too am a man who walks

---

a 8:1 It is best to view this verse as an extension of 7:29. Chapter and verse breaks are not part of the inspired text but were added centuries later to aid in our study of God's Word.

b 8:2 As translated from the Aramaic and Hebrew Matthew, and implied in the Greek.

c 8:3 The word *leprosy* was used for various skin disorders. For Jesus to touch a leper was to render him ceremonially unclean, but Jesus wasn't defiled by touching the leper—the leper was healed!

d 8:4 Or "as a testimony to them." See Leviticus 13–14 for the prescribed ritual for the cleansing of a leper.

e 8:5 Or "centurion."

f 8:5 Implied in the narrative.

g 8:6 As translated from the Aramaic and Hebrew Matthew. The Greek is "servant."

h 8:8–9 Implied in the narrative.

under authority and have authority over soldiers who serve under me. I can tell one to go and he'll go, and another to come and he'll come. I order my servants and they'll do whatever I ask. So I know that all you need to do is to stand here and command healing over my son and he will be instantly healed."

¹⁰Jesus was astonished when he heard this and said to those who were following him, **"He has greater faith than anyone I've encountered in Israel! ¹¹Listen to what I am about to tell you. Multitudes of non-Jewish people will stream from the east and the west, to enter into the banqueting feast with Abraham, Isaac, and Jacob in the heavenly kingdom. ¹²But many Israelites, born to be heirs of the kingdom, will be turned away and banished into the darkness where there will be bitter weeping and unbearable anguish."***a*

¹³Then Jesus turned to the Roman officer and said, **"Go home. All that you have believed for will be done for you!"** And his son was healed at that very moment.

Jesus Heals Everyone in Capernaum

¹⁴Then Jesus went into Peter's home and found Peter's mother-in-law bedridden, severely ill with a fever. ¹⁵The moment Jesus touched her hand she was healed! Immediately she got up and began to make dinner for them.

¹⁶That evening the people brought to him many who were demonized. And by Jesus only speaking a word of healing over them, they were totally set free from their torment,*b* and everyone who was sick received their healing! ¹⁷In doing this, Jesus fulfilled the prophecy of Isaiah:

> **He put upon himself our weaknesses,***c*
> **And he carried away our diseases and made us well.**

---

a 8:12 Or "gnashing of teeth." See also Job 16:9, Psalm 35:16, 37:12, and 112:10, and Jeremiah 9:9–14.

b 8:16 Matthew gives us five instances of setting the demonized free: 8:16, 9:32–34, 12:22, 15:22–28, and 17:18.

c 8:17 The Aramaic "wounds" or "sores." See Isaiah 53:4.

[18]At the sight of large crowds gathering around him, Jesus gave orders to his disciples to get ready to sail back over to the other side of the lake.[a] [19]Just then, a religious scholar[b] approached him and said, "Teacher, I'll follow you wherever you go!"

[20]Jesus replied, **"Foxes have dens, birds have nests, but the Son of Man[c] has no true home in this world."[d]**

[21]Then another man spoke up and said, "Lord, I'll follow you, but first I must take care of my aged father and bury him when he dies."[e]

[22]But Jesus said to him, **"Now is the time to follow me, and let those who are dead bury their own dead."[f]**

Jesus Calms a Storm

[23]They all got into a boat and began to cross over to the other side of the lake. And Jesus, exhausted, fell asleep in the bow.[g] [24]Suddenly a violent storm[h] developed, with waves so high the boat was about to be swamped. Yet Jesus continued to sleep soundly. [25]The disciples woke him up, saying, "Save us, Lord! We're going to die!"[i]

[26]But Jesus reprimanded them. **"Why are you gripped with fear?[j]**

---

a 8:18 This was the eastern bank of the Lake of Galilee, located on the Syrian side.

b 8:19 Or "expert of the Law (scribe)." These were the top religious scholars among the Pharisees, whose occupation was the systematic study of the Law of Moses.

c 8:20 Or "this True Man." See Daniel 7:13–14.

d 8:20 Or "no place to lay my head (homeless)."

e 8:21 Or "But first let me go bury my father." This is a figure of speech for saying, "I can't follow you, but I will after my father dies."

f 8:22 Jesus requires that following him supersede any cultural or religious duty. Jewish culture in the time of Jesus gave the family the responsibility of a re-interment of the bones of the deceased into an ossuary one year after death. It is possible that this man's father had passed away but the year had not yet completed. He was saying, "I'll follow you after this year is completed." Jesus is not telling him to dishonor his father by not doing a burial, but that the custom of waiting a year (tradition) must never trump following him. He is telling the man that the spiritually dead are capable of burying the dead, so nothing should keep anyone from following him.

g 8:23 Implied in the context.

h 8:24 Or "earthquake." This could have been a temblor that caused tidal waves that swamped their boat. Most expositors equate this instead to the shaking of a violent storm.

i 8:25 See Psalm 44:23.

j 8:26 Or "Why are you so cowardly, you of such little faith?" Jesus is implying that if they had faith, they could have commanded the storm to be stilled and it would happen.

Where is your faith?" Then he stood up and rebuked[a] the storm and said, **"Be still!"** And instantly it became perfectly calm.[b]

²⁷The disciples were astonished by this miracle and said to one another, "Who is this Man? Even the wind and waves obey his Word."

Jesus Sets Free Two Demonized Men

²⁸When they arrived on the other side of the lake, in the region of the Gadarenes,[c] two demonized men confronted Jesus. They lived among the tombs of a cemetery and were considered so extremely violent that no one felt safe passing through that area. ²⁹The demons screamed at Jesus, shouting, "Son of God, what do you want with us?[d] Leave us alone! Have you come to torment us before the appointed time?"

³⁰There was a large herd of pigs feeding nearby, ³¹so the demons pleaded, "If you cast us out, send us into that herd of pigs." ³²Jesus commanded, **"Then go!"** And at once the demons came out of the men and went into the pigs.[e] Then the entire herd of crazed pigs stampeded down the steep slope and fell into the water and drowned.

³³The men who were herding the pigs fled to the nearby town and informed the people of all that had happened to the demonized men. ³⁴Then everyone from the town went out to confront Jesus and urged him to go away and leave them alone.[f]

a 8:26 This is the same Greek word that is used when Jesus rebuked demons.

b 8:26 See Psalms 89:9 and 107:23–30.

c 8:28 There are three possible locations for the region of the Gadarenes. 1) It could be only a few miles from the city of Gadara (modern Um Qeis). Gadara means "thorn hedge." 2) The du Tillet translation of Hebrew Matthew has "the region of the Girgashites." 3) Other scholars have concluded that it is the region near the town of Gergesa.

d 8:29 The demons immediately sensed the true identity of Jesus and knew a day of judgment was coming for them. Sadly, many people today have yet to realize who Jesus is and that there is a coming day of judgment for them.

e 8:32 How amazing that Jesus answered the request of the demons. How much more will he answer your prayers. This mass exorcism is an astonishing miracle demonstrating the authority and power of Jesus. It is also amazing that the people of the town didn't ask Jesus to remain with them. The one who can deliver two men from demonic power can also deliver a city.

f 8:34 It is possible that the people of this region worshipped the Sow Goddess, called "Nut" in Egypt. In Rome she was called "Maia," from which we get the month of May. The swine herders were possibly soothsayers and shamans. The mass suicide of these pigs proved that the Son of God had authority over the principality of that region that confronted him the moment he came into their region.

Nine

Forgiveness and Healing

[1]Jesus got into the boat and returned to what was considered his home-town, Capernaum.[a] [2]Just then some people brought a paraplegic man to him, lying on a sleeping mat. When Jesus perceived the strong faith within their hearts, he said to the paralyzed man, **"My son, be encouraged, for your sins have been forgiven."**[b]

[3]These words prompted some of the religious scholars who were present to think, *Why, that's nothing but blasphemy!*

[4]Jesus supernaturally perceived their thoughts, and said to them, **"Why do you carry such evil in your hearts? [5]Which is easier to say, 'Your sins are forgiven,' or, 'Stand up and walk!'?**[c] **[6]But now, to convince you that the Son of Man has been given authority to forgive sins, I say to this man, 'Stand up, pick up your mat, and walk home.'"** [7]Immediately the man sprang to his feet and left for home.

[8]When the crowds witnessed this miracle, they were awestruck.[d] They shouted praises to God because he had given such authority to human beings.

---

a 9:1 Implied in the text. Jesus had moved from Nazareth to Capernaum. See Matthew 4:13.
b 9:2 The Hebrew Matthew reads, "By the faith of the Mighty One your sins are forgiven." See also Psalm 103:3.
c 9:5 It is easy for anyone to say, "Your sins are forgiven," for that cannot be proven. But if someone were to tell a paralyzed man to stand up, and he didn't stand up, that would prove the person is a fraud. Jesus didn't do the easy thing without accomplishing the hard thing, the miracle of healing. Forgiveness and healing both flow from Jesus Christ.
d 9:8 Or "seized with fear."

Jesus Calls Matthew to Follow Him

[9]As Jesus left Capernaum he came upon a tax-collecting station, where a traitorous Jew was busy at his work,[a] collecting taxes for the Romans. His name was Matthew. **"Come, follow Me,"** Jesus said to him. Immediately Matthew jumped up and began to follow Jesus.

[10]Later, Jesus went to Matthew's home to share a meal with him. Many other tax collectors and outcasts of society were invited to eat with Jesus and his disciples.

[11]When those known as "the Separated Ones" saw what was happening, they were indignant, and they kept asking Jesus' disciples, "Why would your Master dine with such lowlifes?"

[12]When Jesus overheard this, he spoke up and said, **"Healthy people don't need to see a doctor, but the sick[b] will go for treatment."** [13]Then he added, **"Now you should go and study the meaning of the verse:**

> **I want you to show mercy, not just offer me a sacrifice.[c]**

For I have come to invite the outcasts of society and sinners, not those who think they are already on the right path."[d]

Jesus Brings a New Reality

[14]The disciples of John the Baptizer approached Jesus with this question: "Why is it that we and the "separated ones" fast regularly, but not your disciples?"

---

a 9:9 Or "sitting at his tax-collecting booth." Matthew means "gift of God." He was also known as Levi, which means "joined." It is possible that he took the name Matthew after becoming a believer.

b 9:12 The Hebrew word for "sick" can also mean "evil."

c 9:13 See Hosea 6:6. To "offer a sacrifice" would be a metaphor for placing strict obedience to the law over the triumph of mercy's kiss in our dealings with others. Sadly, many religious people today read this as "I desire religious exactness, not mercy." Transforming ministry shows unmerited mercy to the "sick."

d 9:13 The obvious implication Jesus is making is that all are sinners who need to come to him for salvation.

¹⁵Jesus replied, "How can the sons of the bridal chamber[a] grieve when the Bridegroom is next to them? But the days of fasting will come when the Bridegroom is taken away from them. ¹⁶And who would mend worn-out clothing with old, worn-out fabric? When the new cloth shrinks it will rip, making the hole worse than before. ¹⁷And who would pour fresh, new wine into an old wineskin? Eventually the wine will ferment and make the wineskin burst, losing everything—the wine is spilled and the wineskin ruined. Instead, new wine is always poured into a new wineskin so that both are preserved."[b]

Jesus Heals and Raises the Dead

¹⁸While Jesus was still speaking, an influential Jewish leader[c] approached and knelt before him, saying, "Help me! My daughter has just died. Please come and place your hand upon her so that she will live again." ¹⁹So Jesus and his disciples got up and went with him.

²⁰Suddenly, a woman came from behind Jesus and touched the tassel of his prayer shawl for healing.[d] She had been suffering from continual bleeding for twelve years, but had faith that Jesus could heal her.[e] ²¹For she kept saying to herself, *If I could only touch his prayer shawl I would be healed.*

a 9:15 See Song of Songs 1:4. These sons of the bridal chamber are "Shulamites," lovers of God.

b 9:17 The teaching of Jesus is the new wine and the new cloth. What Jesus taught cannot patch up the old religious system, nor can it be contained in a wineskin of worn-out traditions. It is new, exhilarating, and powerful. It must be poured into a heart made new. The new and the old are not meant to be together. Jesus makes all things new. He didn't come to reform Judaism, but to form a twice-born company of people.

c 9:18 This was Jairus, who was the leader of the Jewish synagogue and possibly even a member of the Sanhedrin. See Mark 5:21–23 and Luke 8:40–42. The interwoven miracles of the daughter being raised from the dead and the woman being healed symbolize Israel and the church. Israel is the "dead daughter" that Jesus will soon raise to new life. On his way to raise her from the dead, he encountered a woman and healed her. The church is the healed woman. The girl, according to Jesus, was only "sleeping." He will come back to Israel, but on his way, he will heal the woman who touched him by faith. Jesus touched the girl, and the woman touched Jesus. The girl lived twelve years, then died. The woman had been dying twelve years, and then she lived.

d 9:20 Or "for salvation." The blue tassel on the corner of the prayer shawl was said to symbolize all commandments and promises of God. See Numbers 15:38–40. The Hebrew word for "fringe" or "border (of a garment)" can also mean "wing." Some have interpreted Malachi 4:2 ("healing in his wings") as a reference to the tassels of the prayer shawl.

e 9:20 Implied in the text.

²²Just then Jesus turned around and looked at her and said, **"My daughter, be encouraged. Your faith has healed you."**ᵃ And instantly she was healed!

²³When Jesus finally entered the home of the Jewish leader, he saw a noisy crowd of mourners, wailing and playing a funeral dirge on their flutes. ²⁴He told them, **"You must leave, for the little girl is not dead; she's only asleep."** Then everyone began to ridicule him.

²⁵After he made the crowd go outside, he went into the girl's room and gently took hold of her hand. She immediately stood to her feet! ²⁶And the news of this incredible miracle spread everywhere.

Jesus Opens Blind Eyes

²⁷As Jesus left the house, two blind men began following him, shouting out over and over, "Son of David,ᵇ show us mercy and heal us!" ²⁸And they followed him right into the house where Jesus was staying.ᶜ So Jesus asked them, **"Do you believe that I have the power to restore sight to your eyes?"** They replied, "Yes Lord, we believe!"

²⁹Then Jesus put his hand over their eyes and said, **"You will have what your faith expects!"** ³⁰And instantly their eyes opened—they could see! Then Jesus warned them sternly, **"Make sure that you tell no one what just happened!"** ³¹But unable to contain themselves, they went out and spread the news everywhere!

Jesus Heals the Mute

³²While they were leaving, some people brought before Jesus a man with a demon spirit who couldn't speak. ³³Jesus cast the demon out of him, and

---

a 9:22 Or "saved you."

b 9:27 This phrase is an obvious Messianic term. The blind men are hoping that Jesus is the Messiah who will come and restore sight to the blind. See Isaiah 29:18, 35:5–6, and 42:7. Other than the wise men at Jesus' birth, these two blind men were the first to recognize Jesus as King.

c 9:28 This was most likely in Capernaum.

immediately the man began to speak plainly.[a] The crowds marveled in astonishment, saying, "We've never seen miracles like this in Israel!"[b] [34]But the "separated ones"[c] kept saying, "The chief of demons is helping him drive out demons."

Workers for the Harvest

[35]Jesus walked throughout the region[d] with the joyful message of God's kingdom realm. He taught in their meeting houses, and wherever he went he demonstrated God's power by healing every kind of disease and illness.

[36]When he saw the vast crowds of people, Jesus' heart was deeply moved with compassion, because they seemed weary and helpless, like wandering sheep without a shepherd. [37]He turned to his disciples and said, **"The harvest is huge and ripe! But there are not enough harvesters to bring it all in. [38]As you go, plead with the Owner of the Harvest to thrust out[e] many more reapers to harvest his grain!"**

a 9:33 Implied in the text.

b 9:33 Matthew 8 and 9 give us ten miracles that Jesus performed as signs to prove that he is the Messiah. Five are found in each chapter. In chapter 8 we find the leper healed, the military captain's son healed, Simon's mother-in-law healed, the raging storm stilled, and two demon-possessed men set free. In chapter 9 we find the paraplegic man healed, the woman with constant bleeding healed, Jairus's daughter raised from the dead, and two blind men given sight. These signs demonstrated Jesus' authority and power over sickness, storms, Satan, and death.

c 9:34 Or "Pharisees," which means "separated ones."

d 9:35 Or "in all the towns and villages."

e 9:38 The Greek word *ekballo* is used many times in the gospels for driving out or casting out demons. The Lord of the Harvest must cast the laborers out into the harvest fields.

Ten

Jesus Sends Out His Twelve Apostles

[1] Jesus gathered his twelve[a] disciples and imparted to them authority to cast out demons and to heal every sickness[b] and every disease.

[2] Now, these are the names of the first twelve apostles: first, Simon, who is nicknamed Peter, and Andrew, his brother. And then James[c] and John, sons of Zebedee. [3] Next were Phillip and Bartholomew;[d] then Thomas and Matthew, the tax collector; Jacob the son of Alphaeus; Thaddeus;[e] [4] Simon, the former member of the Zealot party,[f] and Judas the locksmith, who eventually betrayed Jesus.[g]

[5] Jesus commissioned these twelve to go out into the ripened harvest fields[h] with these instructions: **"Don't go into any non-Jewish or Samaritan**

---

a 10:1 The number twelve speaks of governmental authority. Israel had twelve tribes, and Jesus chose twelve disciples. Only after Jesus gave them this authority were they called apostles. The authority Jesus gave them is what he had demonstrated over the previous five chapters of Matthew. After Christ's resurrection he reminded them, as he sent them again to the nations, that "all authority has already been given to you." Here Jesus makes these twelve men the answer to their own prayers for the Lord of the Harvest to send out more reapers.

b 10:1 The Aramaic word is "ailment" or "affliction."

c 10:2 Or "Jacob." Although James is his Greek name, the Hebrew and Aramaic is Jacob.

d 10:3 Bartholomew is likely another name for Nathaniel. See John 1:45.

e 10:3 Or "Lebbaeus."

f 10:4 Or "the patriot." The Zealot party was also known as the Daggar party. Some manuscripts read "Simon the Canaanite."

g 10:4 The name Judas is actually Judah. Iscariot is not his last name, but could be taken from the name of the town, Kerioth, twelve miles south of Hebron. But more plausibly, Iscariot is taken from a Hebrew word meaning "lock," Judah being a locksmith. He likely was the chosen to lock the collection bag, which means he had the key and could pilfer the fund at will. It is his sad history that he wanted to lock up Jesus and control him for his own ends.

h 10:5 Implied in the context.

territory.[a] [6]Go instead and find the lost sheep[b] among the people of Israel. [7]And as you go, preach this message: 'Heaven's kingdom realm is accessible, close enough to touch.'[c] [8]You must continually bring healing to lepers and to those who are sick,[d] and make it your habit to break off the demonic presence from people,[e] and raise the dead back to life. Freely[f] you have received the power of the kingdom,[g] so freely release it to others. [9]You won't need a lot of money.[h] [10]Travel light,[i] and don't even pack an extra change of clothes in your backpack. Trust God for everything, because the one who works for him deserves to be provided for.

[11]"Whatever village or town you enter, search for a godly[j] man who will let you into his home until you leave for the next town. [12]Once you enter a house, speak to the family there and say, 'God's blessing of peace be upon this house!' [13]And if those living there welcome you, let your peace come upon the house. But if you are rejected, that blessing of peace will come back upon you. [14]And if anyone doesn't listen to you and rejects your message, when you leave that house or town, shake the dust off your

a 10:5 Or "Don't go on the paths of the non-Jewish people."
b 10:6 The Hebrew Matthew is "the sheep who have strayed from the house of Israel."
c 10:7 The Hebrew Matthew and a few Greek manuscripts add the call to repentance with the word "Repent (turn from sin and turn to God), for the kingdom of heaven approaches."
d 10:8 Or "the weak."
e 10:8 The Aramaic is "Cure the insane."
f 10:8 That is, don't charge for preaching the gospel.
g 10:9 Implied in the context.
h 10:9 Or "Don't take gold, silver, or copper." The Hebrew Matthew is "Don't heap up silver and gold in your money belts." The Aramaic has the nuance of more than not taking money, but not going after the accumulation of money by using God's anointing.
i 10:10 Or "Don't take sandals or a staff," which is likely a figure of speech for "Travel light." The reason Jesus tells his disciples to leave their things behind is that they already had what was most important. Our "money" or wealth is in the kingdom realm of God. Our "clothing" is the garment of righteousness we wear in Christ. Our "backpack" points to our past experiences, which we tend to carry as weights on our backs. We leave our past behind since it no longer exists in Christ. Our "shoes" become a picture of the good news we walk in as we experience his continual peace. Our "staff" is a symbol of authority, and we take with us no other authority but Christ's. We can leave it all behind since we take it all with us in Christ.
j 10:11 Or "worthy" or "honorable"; that is, "deserving of your confidence." The "worthy" man would be one who welcomed the disciples into his home, providing hospitality to them.

feet as a prophetic act that you will not take their defilement with you.[a] [15]Mark my words, on the day of judgment the wicked people who lived in the land of Sodom and Gomorrah will have a lesser degree of judgment than the city that rejects you, for the people of Sodom and Gomorrah did not have the opportunity that was given to them![b] [16]Now, remember, it is I who sends you out, even though you feel vulnerable as lambs going into a pack of wolves. So be as shrewd as snakes yet as harmless[c] as doves."

Jesus Warns His Apostles of Persecution

[17]"Be on your guard! For there will be those who will betray you before their religious councils and brutally beat you with whips in their public gatherings.[d] [18]And because you follow me, they will take you to stand trial in front of rulers and even kings as an opportunity to testify of me before them and the unbelievers.[e] [19]So when they arrest you, don't worry about how to speak or what you are to say, for the Holy Spirit will give you at that very moment the words to speak. [20]It won't be you speaking but the Spirit of your Father repeatedly speaking through you.[f]

[21]"A brother will betray his brother unto death—even a father his child! Children will rise up against their parents and have them put to death. [22]Expect to be hated by all because of my name, but be faithful to the end and you will experience life and deliverance.[g] [23]And when they persecute you in one town, flee to another. But I promise you this: you will not deliver

---

a 10:14 Implied in the historical context of shaking dust off of feet when leaving a city. The "uncleanness" could also refer to any bitter response to the rejection they experienced. They were to "shake it off" before they went to their next assignment.

b 10:15 Implied in the context.

c 10:16 Or "innocent."

d 10:17 Although this can be translated "synagogues," it is actually a gathering of people. No one would be scourged in a synagogue building. See Luke 4:28–30. The Sinaiticus version of Matthew is "courts of justice."

e 10:18 This prophecy of Jesus was fulfilled many times over with the apostles of the Lamb.

f 10:20 See Exodus 4:12.

g 10:22 There is found here one of the Agrapha, quoted from an earlier gospel manuscript that has been lost, which reads, "As often as you fall, rise up, and you will be saved." *Akolouthia of Confession.* (Evans, *The Historical Jesus*; 2004, *supra*, at 213).

all the cities and towns of Israel until the Son of Man will have made his appearance.[a]

²⁴"A student is not superior to his teacher any more than a servant would be greater than his master. ²⁵The student must be satisfied to share his teacher's fate and the servant his master's. If they have called the head of the family 'lord of flies,'[b] no wonder they malign the members of his family.

²⁶"Don't be afraid or intimidated by others, for God will bring everything out into the open and every secret will be told. ²⁷What I say to you in the dark, repeat in broad daylight, and what you hear in a whisper, announce it publicly. ²⁸Don't be in fear of those who can kill only the body but not your soul. Fear only God, who is able to destroy both soul and body in hell. ²⁹You can buy two sparrows for only a copper coin, yet not even one sparrow falls from its nest without the knowledge of your Father. Aren't you worth much more to God than many sparrows? ³⁰⁻³¹So don't worry. For your Father cares deeply about even the smallest detail of your life.[c]

³²"If you openly and publicly acknowledge me, I will freely and openly acknowledge you before my heavenly Father. ³³But if you publicly deny that you know me,[d] I will also deny you before my heavenly Father.

³⁴"Perhaps you think I've come to spread peace and calm over the earth—but my coming will bring conflict and division,[e] not peace. ³⁵Because of me,

>A son will turn against his father,
>A daughter her mother

a 10:23 As translated from the Aramaic, which can also be translated "Those who believe (in hope) until the end will live." The Greek is somewhat ambiguous and reads, "You will not finish going through all the towns of Israel before the Son of Man comes."
b 10:25 Or "Baal-zebub," a derisive term for Satan. There is some evidence that the Hebrew word Baal-zebub could also mean "lord of tricks (trickster)."
c 10:30–31 Or "Even the hairs of your head are numbered."
d 10:33 The Aramaic can be translated "he who blasphemes me."
e 10:34 Or "I have not come to bring peace but a sword." The Aramaic word harba can mean either "sword" or "war." The Greek is "sword (of division)." Either term signifies division.

And against her mother-in-law.[a]

[36]Within your own families you will find enemies.[b]

[37]"Whoever loves father or mother or son or daughter more than me is not fit to be my disciple.[c] [38]And whoever comes to me must follow in my steps and be willing to share my cross and experience it as his own, or he cannot be considered to be my disciple. [39]All who seek to live apart from me will lose it all.[d] But those who let go of their lives for my sake and surrender it all to me will discover true life!

[40]"Whoever receives you receives me, and whoever receives me receives the one who sent me.[e] [41]Whoever receives a prophet because he is God's messenger[f] will share a prophet's reward. And whoever welcomes a good and godly man because he follows me[g] will also share in his reward. [42]And whoever gives a cup of cold water to one of my humble disciples, I promise you, he will not go unrewarded."

---

a 10:35 The Hebrew Matthew adds here, "For there will be five in a house, three against two and two against three, father against son and son against father, and they will stand alone." This is missing from the Greek manuscripts.
b 10:36 See Micah 7:6.
c 10:37 Or "is of no use to me." The Hebrew Matthew is "I am not suitable for him."
d 10:39 Or "Anyone who clings to his own life (soul, self, being)."
e 10:40 Justin Martyr (AD 165) cited this verse but translated it, possibly from an earlier manuscript, "He who hears me hears Him who sent me" (First Apology LXXXII).
f 10:41 Or "in the name of a prophet." See 1 Kings 17:9–24 and 2 Kings 4:9–37.
g 10:41 Or "in the name of a righteous person."

$$Eleven$$

Jesus and John the Baptizer

[1]After Jesus finished giving instructions to his twelve disciples, he went on to minister in different villages throughout the region.

[2]Now, while John the Baptizer was in prison, he heard about what Christ was doing among the people, so he sent his disciples to ask him this question: [3]"Are you really the one prophesied would come, or should we still wait for another?"

[4]Jesus answered them, **"Give John this report:** [5]**'The blind see again, the crippled walk, lepers are cured, the deaf hear, the dead are raised back to life, and the poor and broken now hear of the hope of salvation!'[a]** [6]**And tell John that the blessing of heaven comes upon those who never lose their faith in me[b]—no matter what happens!"**

[7]As they were leaving, Jesus began to speak to the crowd about John. **"What kind of man did you see when you went out into the wilderness? Did you expect to see a man who would be easily intimidated?[c]** [8]**Who was he? Did you expect to see a man decked out in the splendid fashion of the day?[d] Those who wear fancy clothes live like kings in palaces.** [9]**Or did you encounter a true prophet out in the lonely wilderness? Yes, John was a**

---

a 11:5 This fulfills many Old Testament references to the coming of the Messiah, including Isaiah 29:18–19, 35:5– 6, and 61:1. Jesus is assuring John that the message he brings is life and salvation, not judgment and wrath.

b 11:6 The Greek text is literally "Blessed are those who are not offended over me."

c 11:7 Or "a reed shaken by the wind?"

d 11:8 See Matthew 3:4.

prophet like those of the past, but he is even more than that! [10]He was the fulfillment of this Scripture:

> See, I am sending my prophetic messenger[a]
> Who will go ahead of me
> And prepare hearts to receive me.[b]

[11]"For I tell you the truth, throughout history there has never been a man who surpasses John the Baptizer. Yet the least of those who now experience heaven's kingdom realm will become even greater than he. [12]From the moment John stepped onto the scene until now, the kingdom of heaven is entered into by force, and passionate people have taken hold of its power.[c] [13]For all the prophets and the Torah[d] prophesied until John appeared. [14]If you can receive this truth, John is the Elijah who was destined to come. [15]So listen and understand what I'm telling you.[e]

[16]"Don't you understand? How could I describe the people of this generation? You're like children playing games on the playground, yelling at their playmates, [17]'You don't like it when we want to play Wedding! And you don't like it when we want to play Funeral! You will neither dance nor mourn.' [18]Why is it that when John came to you, neither feasting nor drinking wine, you said, 'He has a demon in him!'? [19]Yet when the Son of Man came and went to feasts and drank wine, you said, 'Look at this Man! He is nothing but a glutton and a drunkard! He spends all his time with tax

---

a 11:10 Or "angel."
b 11:10 This is quoted from Malachi 3:1.
c 11:12 Or "The kingdom of heaven is governed by force, and violent ones take hold of it." This is one of the most difficult passages in Matthew to translate from the Greek. An alternate translation of this verse could be "From John the Baptist until now, the realm of heaven's kingdom is being plundered by people who have no legal right to enter in, preventing those with the legal right from enjoying what is theirs."
d 11:13 That is, the first five books of the Bible (Genesis, Exodus, Leviticus, Numbers, and Deuteronomy).
e 11:15 Or "Anyone who has ears to hear, let him hear," an idiom that means "You'd better listen!"

collectors and other affluent sinners.'[a] But God's wisdom will be visibly seen living in those who embrace it."[b]

Jesus Criticizes Unrepentant Cities

[20]Then Jesus began to openly denounce the cities where he had done most of his mighty miracles, because the people failed to turn away from sin and return to God. [21]He said, **"How tragic it will be for the city of Korazin! And how horrible for the city of Bethsaida! For if the powerful miracles that I performed in Korazin and Bethsaida had been done in Tyre and Sidon,[c] they would have humbled themselves and repented, and turned from their sins. [22]Tyre and Sidon[d] will better off on judgment day than you! [23]And Capernaum—do you really think you'll be exalted because of the great miracles I have done there? No! You'll be brought down to the depths of hell[e] because of your rejection of me. For if the miracles I worked in your streets were done in Sodom, it would still be standing today! [24]But I tell you, it will be more bearable for the region of Sodom in the day of judgment than it will be for you."**

Jesus Invites Everyone to Come

[25]Then Jesus exclaimed, **"Father, thank you, for you are Lord, the Supreme Ruler over heaven and earth! And you have hidden the great revelation of your authority from those who are proud and wise in their own eyes. Instead, you have shared it with these who humble themselves. [26]Yes, Father, your plan delights your heart, as you've chosen this way to extend your kingdom—by giving it to those who have become like trusting**

---

a 11:19 As translated from Hebrew Matthew.
b 11:19 Or more literally "Wisdom is vindicated by all her children (Gr. *teknon*)" (some manuscripts, "by her deeds"). The Aramaic word can mean either "servant" (disciple) or "works," which would explain the difference in some Greek manuscripts.
c 11:21 The Hebrew Matthew is "Sodom."
d 11:22 Tyre and Sidon were two Gentile cities on the Mediterranean coast that were known for their wickedness.
e 11:23 See Isaiah 14:13-15.

children.[a] 27You have entrusted me with all that you are and all that you have. No one fully and intimately knows the Son except the Father. And no one fully and intimately knows the Father except the Son. But the Son is able to unveil the Father to anyone he chooses.

28"So everyone, come to me! Are you weary, carrying a heavy burden? Then come to me.[b] I will refresh your life, for I am your oasis.[c] 29Simply join your life with mine.[d] Learn my ways and you'll discover that I'm gentle,[e] humble, easy to please. You will find refreshment and rest in me.[f] 30For all that I require of you will be pleasant[g] and easy to bear."[h]

---

a 11:26 Implied in the immediate context.
b 11:28 Many times Jesus said, "Come after (follow) me," but only here does he say, "Come to me." See Exodus 33:14 and Matthew 23:4.
c 11:28 As translated from the Aramaic.
d 11:29 Or "Bend your neck to my yoke." The metaphor of a yoke is that it joins two animals to work as one. It is not simply work or toil that is the focus here, but union with Christ.
e 11:29 The Aramaic is "tranquil" or "peaceful."
f 11:29 As translated from the Hebrew Matthew. The Aramaic could be translated "Come to me and I will cheer (refresh) you. I am cheerful (refreshing) and humble in heart, and you will find cheer (refreshing) for your soul."
g 11:30 Or "kind (delightful)."
h 11:30 See Psalm 55:22.

Twelve

Jesus, Lord over the Sabbath

¹One Saturday, on the day of rest,ᵃ Jesus and his disciples were walking through a field of wheat. The disciples were hungry, so they plucked off some heads of grain and rubbed them in their handsᵇ to eat. ²But when some of the "separated ones" saw what was happening, they said to him, "Look! Your disciples shouldn't be harvesting grain on the Sabbath!"

³Jesus responded, **"Haven't you ever read what King David and his men did when they were hungry? ⁴They entered the house of Godᶜ and ate the sacred bread of God's presence,ᵈ violating the law by eating bread that only the priests were allowed to eat.**

⁵**"And haven't you read in the Torah that the priests violated the rules of the Sabbath by carrying out their duties in the temple on a Saturday, and yet they are without blame? ⁶But I say to you, there is one here who is even greater than the temple. ⁷If only you could learn the meaning of the words 'I want compassion more than a sacrifice,'ᵉ you wouldn't be condemning my innocent disciples. ⁸For the Son of Man exercises his lordship over the Sabbath."ᶠ**

---

a 12:1 The Hebrew word for Sabbath comes from *shavat*, which is the verb "to rest." What was designed to be a day of rest and intimacy with God and family was now complicated by a host of rules and traditions.

b 12:1 As found in Hebrew Matthew.

c 12:4 That is, the tabernacle. See 1 Samuel 21:1–6. Ancient Jewish tradition states that David did this on a Sabbath day. See also Leviticus 24:5–9.

d 12:4 Or "loaves of presentation." See Ezekiel 44:15–16.

e 12:7 See Hosea 6:6. Mercy is greater than ritual.

f 12:8 Jesus made three startling statements that stunned those who heard him. First he said that he was greater than the temple (v. 6), then that God didn't want sacrifices but mercy (v. 7), and finally that he, the Messiah, was the Lord of the Sabbath. Don't be surprised when Jesus shocks you with truth that is outside your understanding.

⁹Then Jesus left them and went into their Jewish meeting house, where ¹⁰he encountered a man who had an atrophied, paralyzed hand.ᵃ The fault-finding "separated ones" asked Jesus, "Is it permissible to perform a work of healing on the Sabbath, when no one is supposed to work?"ᵇ They only asked him this question because they hoped to accuse him of breaking the Jewish laws.ᶜ

¹¹He answered them, **"If any of you had a lamb that fell into a ditch on the Sabbath, wouldn't you reach out your hand and lift it out? ¹²Isn't a man much more valuable than a lamb? So of course, it's always proper to do miracles,ᵈ even on the Sabbath."**

¹³Then he turned to the man and said, "Hold out your hand!" And as he stretched it out, it was restored, exactly like the other.

¹⁴Immediately the "separated ones" went out and started to scheme about how they would do away with him. ¹⁵Jesus knew what they were thinking, so he left by another way. Massive crowds followed him from there, and he healed all who were sick. ¹⁶However, he sternly warned them not to tell others or disclose his real identity, ¹⁷in order to fulfill the prophecy of Isaiah:ᵉ

> ¹⁸**Take a careful look at my servant,ᶠ my chosen one.**
> **I love him dearly**
> **And I find all my delight in him.ᵍ**
> **I will breathe my Spirit upon him**
> **And he will decree justiceʰ to the nations.**

---

a 12:10 There is a reading given by Jerome and quoted in Nicholson: 46, which inserts here these words, possibly from an older manuscript of Hebrew Matthew: "I was a stonemason working with my hands. Jesus, I beg you to heal me so that I don't have to shamefully beg for food." See Jerome, *Commentary in Matthew* xii:13 (de Santos 23).

b 12:10 Implied in the text.

c 12:10 The Aramaic is "They were like pests who wanted to devour him."

d 12:12 As translated from the Aramaic. The Greek is "to do (morally) good."

e 12:17 See Isaiah 42:1–4.

f 12:18 Or "Here is my son."

g 12:18 The Aramaic is literally "He has sun-shined my being."

h 12:18 Or "judgment."

¹⁹He will not quarrel
Or be found yelling in public.
²⁰He won't brush aside the bruised and broken.
He will be gentle with the weak and feeble,^a
Until his victory releases justice.
²¹And the fame of his name
Will birth hope among the people."^b

Jesus Frees a Demonized Man

²²Then a man was brought before Jesus who had a demon spirit that made him both blind and unable to speak. Jesus healed him instantly, and he could see and talk again! ²³The crowds went wild with amazement as they witnessed this miracle. And they kept saying to one another, "Could this man be the Messiah?"^c

²⁴But when the "separated ones"^d overheard what the people were saying about the miracle, they said, "He casts out demons by the power of Satan,^e the prince of demons!"

²⁵Now, Jesus supernaturally perceived their thoughts and motives, so he confronted them by telling them this parable:^f

"Any kingdom that fights against itself will end up in ruins. And any family or community splintered by strife will fall apart. ²⁶So if Satan casts out Satan, he is making war on himself. How then could his kingdom survive? ²⁷So if Satan empowers me to cast out demons, who empowers your exorcists^g to cast them out? Go ask them, for what they do proves you're

a 12:20 Or "A bruised reed he will not break and a smoldering wick he will not extinguish." The Hebrew Matthew adds a phrase here that corresponds to Isaiah 42: "He will not fail or be discouraged."
b 12:21 Hebrew Matthew is "The islands will wait for his teachings."
c 12:23 Or "Could he be the Son of David," a title used for the Messiah.
d 12:24 Or "Pharisees," which means "separated ones."
e 12:24 Or "Beelzebub (Baal-zebub)," a title used for Satan. See footnote on Matthew 10:25.
f 12:25 As translated from the Hebrew Matthew.
g 12:27 Or "your sons," and by implication, "your followers (who are exorcists)."

wrong in your accusations.[a] 28On the other hand, if I drive out demons by the power of the Spirit of God, then the end of Satan's kingdom has come![b] 29Who would dare enter the house of a mighty man and steal his property? First he must be overpowered and tied up by one who is stronger than he. Then his entire house can be plundered and every possession stolen.

30"So join with me,[c] for if you're not on my side you are against me. And if you refuse to help me gather the spoils, you are making things worse.[d] 31This is why I warn you, for God will forgive people for every sin and blasphemy they have committed except one. There is no forgiveness for the sin of blasphemy against the Holy Spirit. 32If anyone speaks evil of me, the Son of Man, he can be forgiven; but if anyone contemptuously speaks against the Holy Spirit, it will never be forgiven, now or ever!"

Only Good Trees Bear Good Fruit

33"You must determine if a tree is good or rotten. You can recognize good trees by their delicious fruit. But if you find rotten fruit, you can be certain that the tree is rotten. The fruit defines the tree. 34But you who are known as the 'separated ones'[e] are rotten to the core! You've been poisoned by the nature of a venomous snake.[f] How can your words be good and trustworthy if you are rotten within? For what has been stored up in your hearts will be heard in the overflow of your words![g]

---

a 12:27 In other words, to condemn Jesus as working by Satan's power would be to condemn their own exorcists.
b 12:28 As translated from Hebrew Matthew and implied in the Greek. The Greek text, somewhat ambiguously, reads, "Then the kingdom of God has approached." The Hebrew Matthew cohesively fits Jesus' parable in making the conclusion that the end of Satan's kingdom has arrived for he has bound the mighty one (Satan) and ransacked his house (kingdom). Regardless, one indeed implies the other.
c 12:30 Implied in the text. Jesus is saying, "This is a war with no neutrality. Join my side or you will miss the spoils of victory and be forever scattered."
d 12:30 Implied in the text. The Hebrew Matthew is "He who does not join me denies me."
e 12:34 Or "Pharisees," which means "separated ones."
f 12:34 Or "You are the sons of snakes"; that is, their inner identity was like a striking, poisonous viper.
g 12:34 The Hebrew Matthew reads, "Truly the heart awakens and the mouth speaks."

³⁵"When virtue is stored within, the hearts of good and upright people will produce good fruit. But when evil is hidden within, those who are evil will produce evil fruit. ³⁶You can be sure of this: when the day of judgment comes, everyone will be held accountable for every careless word[a] he has spoken.[b] ³⁷Your very words will be used as evidence against you, and your words will declare you either innocent or guilty."

The Sign of Jonah

³⁸Then a few Jewish scholars and "separated ones"[c] spoke up and said, "Teacher, why don't you perform a miraculous sign for us."

³⁹Jesus replied, "Only evil people who are unfaithful to God would demand a sign.[d] There will be no sign given to you except the sign of the prophet Jonah. ⁴⁰For just like Jonah was in the belly of the huge sea creature for three days and three nights, so the Son of Man will be in the heart of the earth for three days and three nights. ⁴¹The people of Nineveh will also rise up on the day of judgment to accuse and condemn this generation.[e] For they all repented when they heard the preaching of Jonah, yet you have refused to repent. And there is one greater than Jonah who is preaching to you today! ⁴²Even the Queen of Sheba[f] will rise up on the day of judgment to accuse and condemn this generation for its unbelief! She journeyed from a far and distant land just to hear the wisdom of King Solomon. Yet now there is one greater than Solomon speaking to you, and you still refuse to listen."

---

a 12:36 Or "worthless word." The Aramaic is "every untrue word."

b 12:36 The Agrapha includes a sentence here, also quoted by Justin Martyr: "In the words I find you saying, in those I will judge you." See Justin Martyr, *Dialogue* 47:5.

c 12:38 Or "Pharisees," which means "separated ones."

d 12:39 After experiencing the many miracles of Jesus' love and power, and hearing his words of grace, for them to demand a further sign is what distinguished that generation as "evil."

e 12:41 The Aramaic is "tribe." The Ninevites (modern Mosul Iraq) were pagans, yet through the preaching of one prophet they converted. The people of Israel had many prophets throughout their history, and the greatest Prophet of all was now preaching to them, yet they refused to listen.

f 12:42 Literally "the queen of the south." See 1 Kings 10:1–13. Sheba is modern-day Yemen.

Demons

[43]"When a demon is cast out of a person, it roams around a dry region, looking for a place to rest, but never finds it. [44]Then it says, 'I'll return to the house I moved out of,' and so it goes back, only to find that the house is vacant, warm, and ready for it to move back in.[a] [45]So it goes looking for seven other demons more evil than itself, and they all enter together to live there. Then the person's condition becomes much worse than it was in the beginning. This describes what will also happen to the people of this evil generation."

Jesus' True Family

[46]While Jesus was still speaking to the crowds, his mother and brothers came and stood outside, asking for him to come out and speak with them. [47]Then someone said, "Look, your mother and brothers are standing outside, wanting to have a word with you." [48]But Jesus just looked at him and said, **"Let me introduce you to my true mother and brothers."** [49]Then gesturing to the disciples gathered around him, he said, **"Look closely, for this is my true family. [50]When you obey my heavenly Father, that makes you a part of my true family."**

---

a 12:44 As translated from the Aramaic. The Greek is "swept clean and put in order."

Thirteen

The Parables of Jesus

[1]Later that day, Jesus left the house and sat by the lakeshore to teach the people. [2]Soon, there were so many people surrounding him that he had to teach sitting in a boat while the large crowd stood on the shore. [3]He taught them many things by using stories, parables that would illustrate spiritual truths,[a] saying:

"Consider this: There was a farmer who went out to sow seeds. [4]As he cast his seeds, some fell along the beaten path and the birds came and ate it. [5]Other seeds fell onto gravel that had no topsoil. The seeds quickly shot up, [6]but when the days grew hot, the sprouts were scorched and withered because they had insufficient roots. [7]Other seeds fell among the thorns and weeds, so when the seeds sprouted, so did the weeds, crowding out the good plants. [8]But other seeds fell on good, rich soil that kept producing a good harvest. Some yielded thirty, some sixty, and some even one hundred times as much as he planted! [9]If you're able to understand this, then you need to respond."[b]

---

a 13:3 The Aramaic and Greek use a word for "parable" that means "a metaphor, allegory, simile, illustration, comparison, figure of speech, riddle, or enigmatic saying that is meant to stimulate intense thought." Throughout Hebrew history wise men, prophets, and teachers used parables and allegories as a preferred method of teaching spiritual truths. Poets would write their riddles and musicians would sing their proverbs with verbal imagery. Jesus never taught the people without using allegory and parables (Matthew 13:34). As a true prophet, Jesus' preferred method of teaching was allegory. To deny the validity of allegorical teaching is to ignore the teaching methods of Jesus, the Living Word. This chapter contains seven parables of Jesus: 1) the parable of the seed, 2)the parable of the wheat and weeds, 3) the parable of the net, 4) the parable of the tiny mustard seed, 5) the parable of yeast, 6) the parable of the the the hidden treasure, and 7) the parable of the costly pearl.

b 13:9 Or "The one with ears to hear should use them." See also v. 43.

¹⁰Then his disciples approached Jesus and asked, "Why do you always speak to people in these hard-to-understand parables?"

¹¹He explained, **"You've been given the intimate experience of insight into the hidden truths and mysteries**^a **of the realm of heaven's kingdom, but they have not. ¹²For everyone who listens with an open heart will receive progressively more revelation**^b **until he has more than enough.**^c **But those who don't listen with an open, teachable heart, even the understanding that they think they have will be taken from them.**^d **¹³That's why I teach the people using parables, because they think they're looking for truth, yet because their hearts are unteachable, they never discover it. Although they will listen to me, they never fully perceive the message I speak. ¹⁴The prophecy of Isaiah describes them perfectly:**

> **Although they listen carefully to everything I speak,**
> **They don't understand a thing I say.**
> **They look and pretend to see,**
> **But the eyes of their hearts are closed.**
> **¹⁵Their minds are dull and slow to perceive,**^e
> **Their ears are plugged and are hard of hearing,**
> **And they have deliberately shut their eyes to the truth.**
> **Otherwise they would open their eyes to see,**
> **And open their ears to hear,**
> **And open their minds to understand.**

---

a 13:11 The Greek word *musterion* is found twenty-seven times in the New Testament and means "secrets" or "mysteries." The mysteries of heaven's kingdom realm are spiritual insights into the nature and ways of God. Jesus Christ can only be fully understood by the spirit, not merely by the intellect of man. Jesus taught his disciples using the cryptic language of parables to move them beyond intellectual abilities and engage the spirit. If the listener had a hunger to learn with an open, teachable heart, then Jesus' words brought life and understanding. We must always be those who push aside our opinions and traditions to glean the deepest meaning of all that Jesus did and taught. See also Job 15:8, Proverbs 3:32, 1 Corinthians 2:14, Colossians 2:2, and Colossians 4:3.

b 13:12 Or "To he who has, more will be given." This is an obvious ellipsis that, in the context, refers to having an open heart to receive the understanding of the mysteries of the kingdom of heaven.

c 13:12 Or "until they habitually super-abound (with understanding)."

d 13:12 As translated from Hebrew Matthew.

e 13:15 The Aramaic is "waterlogged."

Then they would turn to me

And let me instantly heal them.[a]

[16]"But your eyes are privileged, for they see. Delighted are your ears, for they are open to hear all these things.[b] [17]Many prophets and godly people in times past yearned to see these days of miracles that you've been favored to see. They would have given everything to hear the revelation you've been favored to hear. Yet they didn't get to see as much as a glimpse or hear even a whisper.

[18]"Now you are ready to listen to the revelation of the parable of the sower and his seeds:

[19]"The seed that fell on the beaten path represents the heart of the one who hears the message of the kingdom realm[c] but doesn't understand it. The adversary then comes and snatches away what was sown into his heart.

[20]"The seed sown on gravel represents the person who gladly hears the kingdom message,[d] but his experience remains shallow.[e] [21]Shortly after he hears it, troubles and persecutions come because of the kingdom message he received. Then he quickly falls away,[f] for the truth didn't sink deeply into his heart.

[22]"The seed sown among weeds represents the person who receives the message, but all of life's busy distractions, his divided heart, and his ambition for wealth[g] result in suffocating the kingdom message and prevent him from bearing spiritual fruit.[h]

---

a 13:15 See Isaiah 6:9–10.
b 13:16 As translated from the Aramaic. Or "Your eyes have a blessing resting upon them because they see, and your ears because they hear."
c 13:19 The Aramaic can be translated "He hears of the manifestation of the kingdom." It is found also in vv. 20, 21, 22, and 23.
d 13:20 Hebrew Matthew is "the word of the Mighty One."
e 13:20 Implied by the "shallow" soil, representing his shallow interest that doesn't sink spiritual roots into the truth of God.
f 13:21 Or "gets offended" or "is made to stumble."
g 13:22 Or "deceptive riches." See Proverbs 23:4–5.
h 13:22 Hebrew Matthew adds a phrase here: "and the adversary causes him to forget the word of God."

[23]"As for the seed that fell upon good, rich soil, it represents the hearts of people who hear and fully embrace the message of the kingdom realm of heaven. Their lives bear good fruit—some yield a harvest of thirty, sixty, even one hundred times as much as was sown."

The Parable of the Weeds

[24]Then Jesus taught them[a] another parable:

"Heaven's kingdom realm can be compared to a farmer who planted good seed in his field. [25]But at night, when everyone was asleep, an enemy came and planted poisonous weeds[b] among the wheat and ran away. [26]When the wheat sprouted and bore grain, the weeds also appeared. [27]So the farmer's hired hands came to him and said, 'Sir, wasn't that good seed that you sowed in the field? Where did all these weeds come from?'

[28]"He answered, 'This has to be the work of an enemy!'

"They replied, 'Do you want us to go and gather up all the weeds?'

[29]"'No,' he said. 'If you pull out the weeds you might uproot the wheat at the same time. [30]You must allow them both to grow together until the time of harvest. At that time, I'll tell my harvesters to make sure they gather the weeds first and tie them all in bundles to be burned. Then they will harvest the wheat and put it into my barn.'"

The Parable of the Tiny Mustard Seed

[31]Then Jesus taught them another parable:

"Heaven's kingdom realm can be compared to the tiny mustard seed that a man takes and plants in his field. [32]Although the smallest of all the seeds, it eventually grows into the greatest of garden plants, becoming a tree for birds to come and build their nests in its branches."

---

a 13:24 Or "set before them." See also vv. 31 and 33.
b 13:25 Or "darnel" or "rye grass." The Greek word zizanion is a noxious weed ('lolium temelentum') that appears from a distance to look like wheat, but has poisonous black seeds. See Fauna and Flora of the Bible (London: United Bible Societies, 1980), 194.

The Parable of the Yeast

33Then he taught them another parable:

"**Heaven's kingdom realm can be compared to yeast that a woman takes and blends into three measures of flour and then waits until all the dough rises.**"[a]

Prophecy and Parables

34Whenever Jesus addressed the crowds, he always spoke in allegories. He never spoke without using parables. 35He did this in order to fulfill the prophecy:

I will speak to you in allegories.
I will reveal secrets that have been concealed
Since before the foundation of the world.[b]

Jesus Explains the Parables

36Jesus left the crowds and went inside the house where he was staying.[c] Then his disciples approached him and asked, "Please explain the deeper meaning of the parable of the weeds growing in the field of wheat."

37He answered, **"The man who sowed his field with good seed represents me, the Son of Man. 38And the field is the world. The good seeds I sow are the children of the kingdom realm. The weeds are the children of the evil one, 39and the enemy who sows them is the devil. The harvest**

---

a 13:33 These two parables, about the tiny mustard seed and the yeast, both teach of God's kingdom having a small beginning but growing until its influence permeates and prevails into all the earth. The "three measure (Hebrew *seahs*) of flour" was nearly twenty-two kilos, enough to feed three hundred people. What once looked unimpressive rises to impact and feed many. The number three always points to resurrection life.

b 13:35 As translated from the Aramaic. The Hebrew Matthew is "I will speak with riddles from ancient times." See Psalm 78:2 and Proverbs 25:2. A parable has hidden meaning. Everything stands for something else. Jesus interprets and unlocks the meaning of the Word to us.

c 13:36 Implied in the text. This was likely in Capernaum.

points to the end of this age, and the harvesters are God's messengers.[a] [40]As the weeds are bundled up and thrown into the fire, so it will be at the close of the age. [41]The Son of Man will send his messengers, and they will uproot everything out of his kingdom. All the lawless ones and everything that causes sin will be removed. [42]And they will throw them into the fiery furnace, where they will experience great sorrow, pain, and anguish.[b] [43]Then the godly ones will shine like the brightness of the sun[c] in their Father's kingdom realm. If you're able to understand this, then you'd better respond!"

Parables of Hidden Treasure and an Extraordinary Pearl

[44]"Heaven's kingdom realm can be illustrated like this:

"A person discovered that there was hidden treasure in a field. Upon finding it, he hid it again. Because of uncovering such treasure, he was overjoyed and sold all that he possessed to buy the entire field just so he could have the treasure.[d]

[45]"Heaven's kingdom realm is also like a jewel merchant in search of rare pearls. [46]When he discovered one very precious[e] and exquisite pearl, he immediately gave up all he had in exchange for it."[f]

a 13:39 Or "(God's) angels." In both Greek and Hebrew the word *angels* can also refer to human messengers.

b 13:42 Or "gnashing of teeth," a metaphor for despair and torment. The Aramaic can be translated "thrown into the essence of fire." The Aramaic word *athuna* can mean either "furnace" or "essence." See also v. 50.

c 13:43 See Judges 5:31, Song of Songs 6:10, Isaiah 60:1, and Daniel 12:3.

d 13:44 Implied in the text. See also Proverbs 2:4. The most accepted interpretation of this parable is that Jesus is the treasure, but Jesus taught that the field is the world (v.38). The allegory breaks down, for a believer doesn't sell all he has (works) and then buy the world to find Jesus (the treasure). It is more plausible to view the hidden treasure as a symbol of you and me. Jesus is the man who sold all that he owned, leaving his exalted place of glory to come and pay for the sin of the whole world with his own blood just so he could have you, his treasure. Heaven's kingdom realm is experienced when we realize what a great price that Jesus places on our souls, for he gave his sacred blood for us. The re-hiding of the treasure is a hint of our new life, hidden in God. See Ephesians 1:4 and Colossians 3:1–5.

e 13:46 The Aramaic is "unique." Jesus is the merchant. (See Song of Songs 3:6.) You are the exquisite and unique pearl that came from the wounded side of Jesus Christ as his beloved follower. You prompted him to give up all, including his sacred blood, in exchange for having you as his very own. See also Hebrews 12:2.

f 13:46 See Isaiah 43:4.

The Parable of the Fishing Net

⁴⁷"Again, heaven's kingdom realm is like a fisherman who casts his large net into the lake, catching an assortment of different kinds of fish. ⁴⁸When the net was filled, the fishermen hauled it up on the shore, and they all sat down to sort out their catch. They collected the good fish in baskets and threw the bad away. ⁴⁹And so it will be at the close of the age. The messengers*a* will come and separate the evil from among the godly ⁵⁰and throw them into the fiery furnace, where they will experience great sorrow, pain, and anguish. ⁵¹Now do you understand all this?"

"Yes," they replied.

⁵²He responded, **"Every scholar of the Scriptures,*b* who is instructed in the ways of heaven's kingdom realm, is like a wealthy home owner with his house filled with treasures both new and old. And he knows how and when to bring them out to show others."*c***

⁵³Right after Jesus taught this series of parables, he left*d* from there.

Jesus Rejected in His Hometown

⁵⁴When Jesus arrived in his hometown of Nazareth,*e* he began teaching the people in the Jewish meeting house.*f* Everyone was dazed, overwhelmed with astonishment over the depth of revelation they were hearing. They said to one another, "Where did this man get such great wisdom and miraculous

---

a 13:49 Or "angels."

b 13:52 Or "scribe."

c 13:52 Implied in the text. These "new treasures" speak of new insights and understandings that are revealed at the proper time. The "old treasures" speak of truths that have been established, founded upon what God has already revealed. Teachers are to bring forth the revelation of God and his word as treasures to the people. We need both new and old insights.

d 13:53 The Greek word for "left" is *metairo* and means "to depart" or "to be lifted up and taken from one place to another."

e 13:54 Implied in the text.

f 13:54 Or "When Jesus arrived in his own region he taught in their Jewish meeting houses."

powers? ⁵⁵Isn't he just the wood-worker's son?ᵃ Isn't his mother named Mary, and his four brothers James, Joseph, Simon, and Judah? ⁵⁶And don't his sisters all live here in Nazareth? How did he get all this revelation and power?"ᵇ ⁵⁷And the people became offended and began to turn against him.ᶜ

Jesus said, **"There's only one place a prophet isn't honored—his own hometown!"** ⁵⁸And their great unbelief kept him from doing any mighty miracles in Nazareth.

---

a 13:55 The Hebrew Matthew is "blacksmith's son." The Greek word *tekton* can be translated "carpenter," "metal worker," "sculptor," "artisan," "stone worker," or "builder." The people of Jesus' hometown presumed that Joseph was his father, but Jesus had no earthly father, because he was "born of a woman."

b 13:56 Implied in the context. See v. 54.

c 13:57 The Aramaic is "They were suspicious of him." The Hebrew Matthew is "They were confused about him."

Fourteen

John the Baptizer Killed

[1]At that time Herod,[a] the Roman ruler over Galilee, heard reports about Jesus. [2]He told his officials, "This man has to be John the Baptizer who has come back from the dead. That's why he has this power to work miracles."[b]

[3]For Herod had earlier arrested John for confronting him over taking the wife of his brother Philip. He had John thrown in prison and placed in chains [4]because John had repeatedly said to him, "It's not legal or proper for you to be married to Herodias, your sister-in-law!"[c] [5]So Herod wanted John dead, but he was afraid of the crowds who flocked to John because they considered him to be a prophet.

[6]During Herod's birthday celebration, the daughter of Herodias[d] danced before Herod and all his distinguished quests, which greatly pleased the king. [7]So he said to her in front of them all, "I give you my oath, ask of me anything you wish and it will be yours!"

[8]Because she had been instructed by her mother, she said, "I want the head of John the Baptizer here on a platter!"

[9]This grieved the king, but because of his oath in front of all of his guests, [10]he had John beheaded in prison. [11]They brought in his head and

---

a 14:1 This was Herod Antipas, the son of Herod the Great who had the infant boys killed in Bethlehem. See Matthew 2:16. Herod Antipas was the one who Jesus stood before to be judged. See Luke 23:15.

b 14:2 The Aramaic is, "this is why powers are emanating from him." Herod believed that it was the spirit of John working through Jesus, not the Spirit of God.

c 14:4 Herod Antipas wanted to take his brother's wife so he divorced his wife, a Nabatean princess, and Herodias divorced Philip so they could marry each other. This was why John confronted Herod. See Leviticus 18:16.

d 14:6 Josephus, the Jewish historian, notes that her daughter was named Salome.

displayed it to her on a platter, and she then had it shown to her mother.

¹²John's disciples went into the prison and carried his body away and buried it. Then they left to find Jesus and tell him what had happened.

Jesus Feeds the Multitude

¹³On hearing this, Jesus slipped away privately by boat to be alone. But when the crowds discovered he had sailed away, they emerged from all the nearby towns and followed him on foot. ¹⁴So when Jesus landed he had a huge crowd waiting for him. Seeing so many people, his heart was deeply moved with compassion toward them, so he healed all the sick who were in the crowd.[a]

¹⁵Later that afternoon the disciples came to Jesus and said, "It's going to be dark soon and the people are hungry, but there's nothing to eat here in this desolate place. You should send the crowds away to the nearby villages to buy themselves some food."

¹⁶**"They don't need to leave,"** Jesus responded. **"You can give them something to eat."**

¹⁷They answered, "But all we have is five barley loaves and two fish."

¹⁸**"Let me have them,"** Jesus replied. ¹⁹Then he had everyone sit down on the grass as he took the five loaves and two fish. He looked up into heaven, gave thanks to God, and broke the bread into pieces. He then gave it to his disciples, who in turn gave it to the crowds. ²⁰And everyone ate until they were satisfied, for the food was multiplied in front of their eyes![b] They picked up the leftovers and filled up twelve baskets full! ²¹There were about five thousand men who were fed, in addition to many women and children!

Jesus Walks on Water

²²As soon as the people were fed, Jesus told his disciples to get into their boat and to go to the other side of the lake while he stayed behind to dis-

a 14:14 The Aramaic is "He nurtured them in love and cured their frailties."
b 14:20 Implied in the text. The miracle took place as the disciples distributed what they had. Each disciple ended up with a basket full of leftovers.

miss the people. ²³After the crowds dispersed, Jesus went up into the hills to pray. And as night fell he was there praying alone with God.

²⁴But the disciples, who were now in the middle of the lake, ran into trouble, for their boat was tossed about by the high winds and heavy seas.

²⁵At about four o'clock in the morning,ᵃ Jesus came to them, walking on the waves! ²⁶When the disciples saw him walking on top of the water, they were terrified and screamed, "A ghost!"

²⁷Then Jesus said, **"Be brave and don't be afraid. I am here!"**ᵇ

²⁸Peter shouted out, "Lord, if it's really you, then have me join you on the water!"

²⁹**"Come and join me,"**ᶜ Jesus replied.

So Peter stepped out onto the water and began to walk toward Jesus. ³⁰But when he realized how high the waves were, he became frightened and started to sink. "Save me, Lord!" he cried out.

³¹Jesus immediately stretched out his hand and lifted him up and said, **"What little faith you have! Why would you let doubt win?"**

³²And the very moment they both stepped into the boat, the raging wind ceased. ³³Then all the disciples crouched down before him and worshipped Jesus.ᵈ They said in adoration, "You are truly the Son of God!"

³⁴After they crossed over and landed at Gennesaret,ᵉ ³⁵the people living there quickly recognized who he was. They were quick to spread the news throughout the surrounding region that Jesus had come to them. ³⁶So they brought him all their sick, begging him to let them touch the fringe of his robe. And everyone who touched it was instantly healed!ᶠ

---

a 14:25 Or "during the fourth watch of the night (between 3:00 and 6:00 a.m.)."
b 14:27 Or "I AM," which was the name of God used in Exodus 3:14.
c 14:29 Or "Go for it!"
d 14:33 The Greek word used for "worship," *proskuneo,* includes three concepts: to bow, to kiss, and to pay homage (worship). All three are included here.
e 14:34 Gennesaret means "harp." It was known as a lovely and fertile plain south of Capernaum. The Lake of Galilee was also called the Lake of Gennesaret.
f 14:36 See also Matthew 9:21–22. Mark 3:10, and Luke 6:19. The power of God exuding from Jesus was so incredible that merely touching his prayer shawl (or cloak) would bring instant healing. This same power is available to the church today, for Christ, the healer, lives in every believer. See also Acts 19:12.

Jesus Breaks Religious Traditions

[1]Then the "separated ones" and religious scholars[a] came from Jerusalem and approached Jesus with this question: [2]"Why do your disciples ignore the traditions of our elders? For example, they don't ceremonially wash their hands before they eat bread."

[3]Jesus answered, **"And why do you ignore the commandment of God because of your traditions? [4]For didn't God say, 'Honor your father and mother,' and, 'Whoever abuses or insults his father or mother must be put to death?'[b]**

[5]**"But you teach that it's permissible to say to your parents when they are in financial need, 'Whatever gift you would have received from me I can keep for myself, since I dedicate it as an offering to God.' [6]This doesn't honor your father or mother. And you have elevated your tradition above the words of God. [7]Frauds and hypocrites! Isaiah described you perfectly when he said:**

> [8]**These people honor me only with their words,**
> **For their hearts are so very distant from me.**
> [9]**They pretend to worship me,**
> **But their worship is nothing more**
> **Than the empty traditions of men."[c]**

a 15:1 Or "scribes," considered to be experts in interpreting Jewish laws.
b 15:4 Exodus 20:12; 21:17; Leviticus 20:9.
c 15:9 See Isaiah 29:13.

¹⁰Then Jesus turned to the crowd and said, **"Come, listen and open your heart to understand. ¹¹What truly contaminates a person is not what he puts into his mouth but what comes out of his mouth. That's what makes people defiled."**

¹²Then his disciples approached him and said, "Don't you know that what you just said offended the 'separated ones'?"ᵃ

¹³Jesus replied, **"Every plant that my heavenly Father didn't plant is destined to be uprooted. ¹⁴Stay away from them,ᵇ for they're nothing more than blind guides. Do you know what happens when a blind man pretends to guide another blind man? They both stumble into a ditch!"**

¹⁵Peter spoke up and said, "Will you explain to us what you mean by your parable?"

¹⁶Jesus said, **"Even after all that I've taught you, you still remain clueless? ¹⁷Is it hard to understand that whatever you eat enters the stomach only to pass out into the sewer? ¹⁸But what comes out of your mouth reveals the core of your heart. Words can pollute, not food. ¹⁹You will find living within an impure heart evil ideas, murderous thoughts, adultery, sexual immorality, theft, lies, and slander.ᶜ ²⁰That's what pollutes a person. Eating with unwashed hands doesn't defile anyone."**

A Lebanese Woman's Faith

²¹Then Jesus left and went north into the non-Jewish region of Lebanon.ᵈ ²²He encountered there a Canaanite womanᵉ who screamed out to him, "Lord, Son of David, show mercy to me! My daughter is horribly afflicted by

---

a 15:12 Or "Pharisees," which means "separated ones."
b 15:14 The Aramaic is "Let them remain blind! For they are nothing more than blind leaders of the blind."
c 15:19 Or "blasphemies."
d 15:21 Or "Tyre and Sidon," both cities of Lebanon.
e 15:22 The Hebrew Matthew is "a Canaanite merchant woman." Canaan included the region of modern-day Lebanon. Canaanite refers to a non-Jewish person who lived in that region. It was in this very region that a woman named Jezebel established Baal worship. Now Jesus heals a woman and brings her into the true worship of God.

a demon that torments her." ²³But Jesus never answered her. So his disciples said to him, "Why do you ignore this woman who is crying out to us?"ᵃ

²⁴Jesus said, **"I've only been sent to the lost sheep of Israel."** ²⁵But she came and bowed down before him and said, "Lord, help me!"

²⁶Jesus responded, **"It's not right for a man to take bread from his children and throw it out to the dogs."**ᵇ

²⁷"You're right, Lord," she replied. "But even puppies get to eat the crumbs that fall from the prince's table."

²⁸Then Jesus answered her, **"Dear woman, your faith is strong! What you desire will be done for you."** And at that very moment, her daughter was instantly set free from demonic torment.

Jesus Heals Many Others

²⁹After leaving Lebanon, Jesus went to the Lake of Galilee and climbed a hill nearby and sat down. ³⁰Then huge crowds of people streamed up the hill, bringing with them the lame, blind, deformed, mute, and many others in need of healing. They laid them at Jesus' feet and he healed them all.

³¹And the crowds marveled with rapture and amazement, astounded over the things they were witnessing with their own eyes! The lame were walking, the mute were speaking, the crippled were made well, and the blind could see. For three daysᶜ everyone celebrated the miracles as they exalted and praised the God of Israel!

Jesus Feeds Thousands

³²Jesus called his disciples to himself and said, **"I care deeply about all these people, for they've already been with me for three days without food. I**

---

a 15:23 As translated from Hebrew Matthew. The Greek is "The disciples kept begging Jesus to send her away."
b 15:26 Jesus uses a figure of speech and describes the people of Israel as "children" who view the non-Jewish people as "dogs."
c 15:31 Implied in the text. See v. 32.

don't want to send them away fasting or else they may be overcome by weakness on their journey home."

33So the disciples said to him, "Where in the world are we going to find enough food in this desolate place to feed this crowd?"

34**"How many barley loaves do you have?"** Jesus asked.

"Seven," they replied, "and a few small fish."

35So he gave the order, **"Have the people sit down on the grass."** 36Then he took the seven loaves and the fish and gave thanks to God. He broke the bread and gave it to his disciples, who then distributed the food to the crowds. 37When everyone was full and satisfied, they gathered up the leftovers. And from what was once seven loaves and a few fish, they filled seven baskets!a 38There were four thousand men who ate the food Jesus multiplied, and even more including the women and children!

39After dismissing the crowd, Jesus got into the boat and crossed over to the region of Magdala.b

---

a 15:37 The Greek word used here implies a very large basket, possibly the size of a person.
b 15:39 Or "Magadan." This was a place where fish were salted and preserved. Magdala means "tower." Magdala was the town that Mary Magdalene came from. Perhaps during this visit is when they first met.

Sixteen

The Demand for a Sign from Heaven

¹One day some of the "separated ones"[a] and those of the Jewish sect known as the Sadducees[b] approached Jesus, insisting that he prove to them that he was the Messiah. "Show us a supernatural sign from heaven," they demanded.

²Jesus answered, **"You can read the signs of the weather, for you say, 'Red sky at night, sailors delight.' ³And, 'Red sky in the morning, sailors take warning.' You're so adept at forecasting the weather by looking at the sky, but you're absolutely clueless in reading the obvious signs of the times. ⁴A wicked and wayward generation always asks for signs, but the only sign I provide for you will be the sign of Jonah the prophet."**[c] Then he turned away and left them.

The Hypocrisy of the Pharisees and Sadducees

⁵Later, as Jesus and his disciples crossed over to the other side of the Lake of Galilee, the disciples realized they had forgotten to bring any loaves of bread. ⁶Jesus spoke up and said, **"Watch out for the yeast of the 'separated ones' and the Sadducees."**

⁷Thinking Jesus was scolding them over not bringing bread, they

---

a 16:1 Or "Pharisees," which means "separated ones."

b 16:1 Of the three major sects of Judaism of that day (Pharisees, Essenes, and Sadducees), the Sadducees were a small but influential group that philosophically denied the supernatural and gravitated instead toward political control of the people.

c 16:4 The "sign of Jonah" points to Jesus in many ways. Jonah being thrown into the sea points to Christ's death. Being swallowed by the fish for three days points to Christ's burial. And being expelled from the fish speaks of Christ's resurrection and triumph over death, which is the greatest "sign" God could ever give. The resurrected Jesus is the eternal sign that our sins are forgiven.

whispered among themselves. [8]Knowing their thoughts, Jesus said to them, **"You have such little faith! Why are you arguing with one another about having no bread? [9]Are you so slow to understand? Have you forgotten the miracle of feeding the five thousand families and how each of you ended up with a basket full of fragments? [10]And how seven loaves of bread fed four thousand families with baskets left over? [11]Don't you understand? I'm not talking about bread, but I'm warning you to avoid the yeast of the 'separated ones' and the Sadducees."**

[12]Then finally they realized he wasn't talking about yeast found in bread, but the error of the teachings of the "separated ones"[a] and the Sadducees.[b]

Peter's Revelation of Christ

[13]When Jesus came to Caesarea Philippi,[c] he asked his disciples this question: **"What are the people saying about me, the Son of Man? Who do they believe I am?"**

[14]They answered, "Some are convinced you are John the Baptizer, others say you are Elijah reincarnated, or Jeremiah, or one of the prophets."

[15]**"But you—who do you say that I am?"** Jesus asked.

[16]Simon Peter spoke up and said, "You are the Anointed One,[d] the Son of the living God!"

a 16:12 Or "Pharisees," which means "separated ones" (separatists). It is believed that during the time of Jesus there were approximately six thousand Pharisees in Israel. They refused to have dealings with the common people, because there were separated to God. Jesus described them as religious frauds who loved money and wanted to be the final authority on all the doctrines that were taught to the people. They were not all priests, but zealous law keepers who wanted their interpretation of the Scriptures to be the standard in Israel.

b 16:12 The Sadducees (*Tzedukim*) were wealthy aristocrats with political connections to Rome. They did not believe in the afterlife or angels or demons, and they denied the miraculous. It is believed that among them were Jewish converts from the Edomites who were forced to convert to Judaism in 129 BC by John Hyrcanus, the Hasmonean leader of the second century BC. The Sadducees loved Greek (Hellenistic) culture and basically rejected the oral law of the Pharisees. The Herodians would also be considered to be of the Sadducees. You can imagine how Jesus upset both the Pharisees and the Sadducees. Jesus had no difficulty breaking the traditions, taboos, religious teachings, and political loyalties of both Pharisees and Sadducees in order to please his heavenly Father.

c 16:13 This was a beautiful area north of the Lake of Galilee and near Tel-Dan. Located at the foothills of Mount Hermon, it was an ancient Roman city rebuilt by Herod Philip in honor of Tiberius Caesar.

d 16:16 Or "the Christ (Messiah)."

[17]Jesus replied, **"You are favored and privileged Simeon, son of Jonah![a]** **For you didn't discover this on your own, but my Father in heaven has supernaturally revealed it to you.** [18]**I give you the name Peter, a stone.[b] And this truth of who I am will be the bedrock foundation on which I will build my church—my legislative assembly,[c] and the power of death[d] will not be able to overpower it![e]** [19]**I will give you the keys[f] of heaven's kingdom realm to forbid on earth that which is forbidden in heaven, and to release on earth that which is released in heaven."[g]** [20]He then gave his disciples strict orders not to tell anyone that he was God's Anointed One.

Jesus Prophesies His Death and Resurrection

[21]From then on Jesus began to clearly reveal to his disciples that he was destined to go to Jerusalem and suffer injustice[h] from the elders, leading priests, and religious scholars. He also explained that he would be killed and three days later be raised to life again.

a 16:17 Jonah means "dove." Or "Simon, son of John." Simeon means "he who hears." Peter heard the Father's whisper within that Jesus was the Christ. Simeon was his formal Hebrew name. Peter became his identity as Jesus gave him the nickname of "pebble." He is also referred to as "Simon Peter."

b 16:18 Or Keefa, the Aramaic word for "stone" or "pebble." See Matthew 4:18 with footnote. There is an obvious pun only found in the Hebrew Matthew. The Hebrew word for "stone" is *eben*, and the Hebrew word for "build" is *ebeneh*. The Greek text does state that Peter is the "rock" on which the church is built. However, the implication is that it is Peter's revelation from the Father and his confession of Jesus as the Son of God that becomes the "bedrock foundation" for the church. The earliest writings of the church fathers all acknowledge that the Rock is Jesus Christ, not Peter. See Deuteronomy 32:18, 30-31, Psalm 18:46, and Isaiah 8:14, 17:10, 51:1-8.

c 16:18 The Greek word for "church" is *ekklesia* and means "legislative assembly" or "selected ones." This is not a religious term at all, but a political and governmental term that is used many times in classical Greek for a group of people who have been summoned and gathered together to govern the affairs of a city. For Jesus to use this term means he is giving the keys of governmental authority in his kingdom to the church. See R. Scott and H. G. Liddell, *A Greek-English Lexicon*, p. 206; J. H. Thayer, *A Greek-English Lexicon of the New Testament*, p. 196; and Oskar Seyffert, *A Dictionary of Classical Antiquities*, pp. 202-203.

d 16:18 Or "the gates of hell," a metonymy for the power of death.

e 16:18 Or "All the forces of hell will never have the power to win a victory over it!" There is no power of darkness that can stop the advancing church that Jesus builds.

f 16:19 The "keys" are symbols of authority and ruling power. See Isaiah 22:22.

g 16:19 Or "Whatever you bind on earth will have been bound in heaven, and whatever you loose on earth will have been loosed in heaven." Or "That which you forbid on earth must be that which is already forbidden in heaven, and that which you permit on earth must be that which is already permitted in heaven."

h 16:21 The Hebrew Matthew adds, "many scourgings and many mockings."

²²Peter took him aside to correct him privately. He reprimanded Jesus over and over, saying to him, "God forbid, Master! Spare yourself. You must never let this happen to you!"

²³Jesus turned to Peter^a and said, **"Get out of my way, you Satan!^b You are an offense to me,^c because your thoughts are only filled with man's viewpoints and not with the ways of God."**

²⁴Then Jesus said to his disciples, **"If you truly want to follow me, you should at once completely reject and disown your own life. And you must be willing to share my cross and experience it as your own,^d as you continually surrender to my ways. ²⁵For if you choose self-sacrifice and lose your lives for my glory, you will continually discover true life. But if you choose to keep your lives for yourselves, you will forfeit what you try to keep. ²⁶For even if you were to gain all the wealth and power of this world with everything it could offer you—at the cost of your own life—what good would that be? And what could be more valuable to you than your own soul?^e ²⁷It has been decreed that I, the Son of Man, will one day return with my messengers^f and in the splendor and majesty of my Father. And then I will reward each person according to what they have done.^g ²⁸But I promise you, there are some standing here now who won't experience death until they have witnessed the coming of the Son of Man in the presence and the power of the kingdom realm of God!"^h**

---

a 16:23 Or "He turned from Peter and said…"

b 16:23 Or "adversary." Jesus is equating Peter's display of character to that of Satan. Peter was not possessed by Satan, but speaking from Satan's realm and speaking demonic wisdom. See James 3:15. The Hebrew Matthew can be translated "Follow me! Don't quarrel with me, adversary!"

c 16:23 Or "You are laying a trap for me."

d 16:24 The Hebrew Matthew is "offer yourself up to death." The words Jesus spoke were shocking and must be translated as such.

e 16:26 Or "What would a person give in exchange for his life?"

f 16:27 Or "angels."

g 16:27 See Psalm 28:4, Psalm 62:12, and Proverbs 24:12.

h 16:28 Or "when they see the Son of Man appearing to inaugurate his regal reign." This was a prophecy of what was about to take place with Peter, James, and John on the Mountain of Transforming Glory. This promise would be fulfilled as they experienced the power of the kingdom of God and the cloud of glory. Christ's appearing is equated to the power manifested in the cloud that overshadowed Jesus on the Mount of Transfiguration.

Seventeen

Jesus' Glorious Transfiguration

[1]Six days later Jesus took Peter and the two brothers, James and John, and hiked up a high mountain to be alone. [2]Then Jesus' appearance was dramatically altered. A radiant light as bright as the sun poured from his face. And his clothing became luminescent—dazzling like lightning.[a] He was transfigured[b] before their very eyes. [3]Then suddenly, Moses and Elijah appeared,[c] and they spoke with Jesus.

[4]Peter blurted out, "Lord, it's so wonderful that we are all here together! If you want, I'll construct three shrines,[d] one for you, one for Moses, and one for Elijah.[e]

[5]But while Peter was still speaking, a radiant cloud composed of light spread over them, enveloping them all.[f] And God's voice suddenly spoke

---

a 17:2 Or "white as light."

b 17:2 Moses also went up Sinai's mountain and received an impartation of glory. His face shined and had to be veiled. The transfiguration of Jesus is also part of our destiny, for the same Greek word is used twice for believers being transfigured by the renewing of our minds and by the glory of Christ within us that will complete our transformation into Christ's image. See Romans 12:2 and 2 Corinthians 3:18.

c 17:3 Moses represented the law and Elijah represented the prophets. Both Moses and Elijah were associated with Mount Sinai (Horeb), both had a ministry of performing astounding miracles, and both had unusual circumstances surrounding their passing from this life into glory.

d 17:4 Or "tabernacles," which speaks of the booths made to celebrate the Feast of Tabernacles.

e 17:4 The Hebrew Matthew adds this line: "because he (Peter) did not know what he was saying."

f 17:5 See Acts 5:15. The Greek word translated "overshadow" is *episkiazo*, which is used exclusively for the power of the Almighty "overshadowing," such as Mary, who conceived a child supernaturally by God. See also Mark 9:7 and Luke 1:35. This was not a natural shadow created by the light of the sun, but the supernatural overshadowing of God's power. Jesus will appear again in these clouds of glory. See Matthew 16:27, 24:30, and 26:64.

from the cloud, saying, **"This is my dearly loved Son, the constant focus of my delight.**[a] **Listen to him!"**[b]

⁶The three disciples were dazed[c] and terrified by this phenomenon, and they fell facedown to the ground. ⁷But Jesus walked over and touched them, saying, **"Get up and stop being afraid."** ⁸When they finally opened their eyes and looked around, they saw no one else there but Jesus.[d]

⁹As they all hiked down the mountain together, Jesus ordered them, **"Don't tell anyone of the divine appearance**[e] **you just witnessed. Wait until the Son of Man is raised from the dead."**

¹⁰His disciples asked him, "Why do all the religious scholars insist that Elijah must first appear before the Anointed One comes?"

¹¹He answered them, **"They're right. Elijah must come first and restore all things. **¹²**But Elijah has already appeared. And yet they didn't recognize him, so they did to him whatever they pleased. And the Son of Man is destined to suffer the same abuse as what they did to him."**

¹³Then the disciples realized that Jesus was referring to John the Baptizer all along.[f]

Unbelief Hinders Healing

¹⁴They came to where a large crowd had gathered to wait for Jesus.[g] A man came and knelt before him ¹⁵and said, "Lord, please show your tender

a 17:5 Or "He is the one on whom my favor rests."
b 17:5 Or "You must constantly listen to him." See Psalm 2:7 and Isaiah 42:1.
c 17:6 Implied by the Hebrew Matthew, which can be translated "They were asleep and not asleep; they were awake but not awake."
d 17:8 The Greek is quite emphatic: "They saw only him, and him alone."
e 17:9 Or "supernatural vision." The Greek word used here *(horama)* does not refer to an imaginary vision, but an actual one. It points to a theophany, an appearing of God.
f 17:13 Jesus was comparing Elijah with John the Baptist. John was not Elijah reincarnated, but the Spirit upon Elijah was the Spirit upon John. John, the forerunner, ministered in the spirit and power of Elijah. The same anointing of Elijah is present today to restore all things. (See Acts 3:21.) The Bible scholars had properly concluded that Elijah must come first, but failed to interpret it figuratively. This is often repeated today with biblical prophecies. We need the Spirit of Christ to help us understand even the basic truths of the Bible.
g 17:14 Implied in the text.

mercy toward my son. He has a demon who afflicts him.[a] He has epilepsy, and he suffers horribly from seizures. He often falls into the cooking fire or into the river.[b] [16]I brought him to your followers, but they weren't able to heal him."

[17]Jesus replied, **"Where is your faith? Can't you see how wayward and wrong this generation is?[c] How much longer do I stay with you and put up with your doubts? Bring your son to me."**

[18]Then Jesus rebuked the demon and it came out of him and the boy was instantly healed!

[19]Later the disciples came to him privately and asked, "Why couldn't we cast out the demon?"

[20]He told them, **"It was because of your lack of faith. I promise you, if you have faith inside of you no bigger than the size of a small mustard seed, you can say to this mountain, 'Move away from here and go over there,' and you will see it move![d] There is nothing you couldn't do![e]** [21]**But this kind of demon is cast out only through prayer and fasting."[f]**

Jesus Prophesies Again of His Death and Resurrection

[22]When they all gathered together[g] in Galilee, Jesus said to them, **"The Son of Man is going to be betrayed and turned over to his enemies.** [23]**They will kill him and in three days he will be resurrected."** When the disciples heard these words they were devastated.

---

a 17:15 Although not in the Greek text, it is implied in the context (v. 18). The Hebrew Matthew states three times in this pericope (vv. 15, 18, 21) that the boy had a demon.
b 17:15 The Hebrew Matthew is "He grinds his teeth and foams at the mouth."
c 17:17 The Hebrew Matthew adds a sentence here: "Woe to those who deny me!"
d 17:20 Jesus compares faith to a small seed that grows into a large shrub. Faith will grow as it feeds on spiritual truth found in the Bible. A mountain can also be a symbol of a kingdom. Mountain-moving faith brings the power of God's kingdom to the earth. See also 1 Corinthians 13:2.
e 17:20 Or "Nothing will be beyond your power." The Aramaic can be translated "Nothing is higher or stronger than you."
f 17:21 As translated from the Hebrew Matthew, Aramaic, and some Greek manuscripts. Many reliable Greek manuscripts do not have this verse, and it is not included in many modern translations.
g 17:22 The Greek word is "twisted together like strands of a rope."

The Miracle of a Coin in a Fish's Mouth

[24]After they arrived in Capernaum, the collectors of the temple tax approached Peter and asked, "Does your teacher pay the tax for the upkeep of the temple, like the rest of us?"[a]

[25]"Of course he does," Peter answered.

When Peter walked into the house, and before he had a chance to speak, Jesus spoke up and said, **"Peter, I have a question for you. Who pays tolls or taxes to a king? Is tax collected from the king's own children, or from his subjects?"**

[26]"From his subjects," Peter answered.

Jesus replied, **"That's right. The children get off free without paying taxes. [27]But so that we don't offend them, go to the lake and throw out your hook, and the first fish that rises up[b] will have a coin in its mouth. It will be the exact amount you need to pay the temple tax for both of us."[c]**

---

a 17:24 This was known as "head tax." See also Exodus 30:13–16, Exodus 38:26, and Nehemiah 10:32–33. The word *pay* (vv. 24, 25, 27) is the same word Jesus spoke on the cross, "It is finished (*paid* in full)." Jesus paid it all so that we would be set free.

b 17:27 This miracle is a picture of the death and resurrection of our Lord Jesus. The depth of the sea speaks to us of the depth of suffering Jesus passed through for us on the cross. Note that the fish rose to the surface on its own; it was not "caught," but risen. In the mouth of our Lord Jesus is the full price of our sin debt, for he has declared the work of redemption finished, and our "tax" has been paid in full. Now we have that same message in our mouths.

c 17:27 Peter made a presumptuous statement to the tax collectors that Jesus would pay the temple tax. But Peter didn't ask Jesus first; he just said to them, "Of course!" Yet Jesus still backed up Peter's word and performed a miracle to pay the tax. In this somewhat amusing account, Jesus got Peter "off the hook" by having him hook a fish with the exact amount of the tax for both Jesus and Peter. The children of the King are the true temple of God today. See 1 Corinthians 3:16.

Eighteen

Who Is the Greatest in the Kingdom Realm?

¹At that time the disciples came to ask Jesus, "Who is considered to be the greatest in heaven's kingdom realm?"ᵃ

²Jesus called a toddlerᵇ to his side and said to them, ³**"Learn this well: Unless you dramatically change your way of thinking and become teachable, and learn about heaven's kingdom realm with the wide-eyed wonder of a child, you will never be able to enter in. ⁴Whoever continually humbles himselfᶜ to become like this gentle child is the greatest one in heaven's kingdom realm. ⁵And if you tenderly care for this toddlerᵈ on my behalf, you are tenderly caring for me. ⁶But if anyone abusesᵉ one of these little ones who believe in me, it would be better for him to have a heavy boulder tied around his neck and be hurled into the deepest sea than to face the punishment he deserves!ᶠ**

⁷**"Misery will come to the one who lures people away into sin. Troubles and obstacles to your faith are inevitable, but great devastation will come to the one guilty of causing others to leave the path of righteousness! ⁸If your hand clings to sin, cut it off and throw it away. If your foot continually steps onto sin's path, cut it off and throw it away. For it is better for you to**

ᵃ 18:1 The Aramaic is "Who will reign in the kingdom realm of heaven?"

ᵇ 18:2 Or "little child." The Greek word is *neuter*, either a boy or a girl.

ᶜ 18:4 This means "to see yourself as unimportant in your own eyes."

ᵈ 18:5 The Greek uses the word for hospitality. The "little child" becomes a representative of unimportant people in general. Treating the least with care and respect makes us truly great.

ᵉ 18:6 The Greek word is *skandalizō* and can also mean "to scandalize," "to put a stumbling block before them," "to offend," or "to cause to sin."

ᶠ 18:6 Implied in the text. The Hebrew Matthew adds, "It would be better for him to never have been born!"

enter into heaven crippled and maimed than to have both hands and both feet and be thrown into eternal fire. [9]And if your eye is always focusing on sin, pluck it out and throw it away. For it is better for you to enter into heaven with one eye than to be thrown into hell fire with two.[a]

[10]"Be careful that you not corrupt[b] one of these little ones. For I can assure you that in heaven each of their angelic guardians[c] have instant access[d] to my heavenly Father."

A Parable of the Lost Lamb

[11]"The Son of Man has come to give life to anyone who is lost.[e] [12]Think of it this way: If a man owns a hundred sheep and one lamb wanders away and is lost, won't he leave the ninety-nine grazing on the hillside and go out and thoroughly search for the one lost lamb? [13]And if he finds his lost lamb, he rejoices over it, more than over the ninety-nine who are safe.[f] [14]Now you should understand that it is never the desire of your heavenly Father that a single one of these humble believers[g] should be lost."[h]

Restoring Broken Relationships

[15]"If your fellow believer sins against you,[i] you must go to that one privately and attempt to resolve the matter. If he responds, your relationship is restored.[j] [16]But if his heart is closed to you, then go to him again, taking

---

a 18:9 Although the language Jesus uses is hyperbolic, the drastic measures He instructs us to take in order to stay pure remain valid. The last phrase is literally "into the Gehenna of fire!"

b 18:10 As translated from the Aramaic, which uses a figure of speech ("to bring down") that is best translated "to corrupt or degrade." The Greek is "despise," or "look down upon."

c 18:10 As translated from the Aramaic. The Greek is simply "angels."

d 18:10 Or "who always see the face of my heavenly Father."

e 18:11 As translated from the Hebrew Matthew, the Aramaic, and a few Greek texts. Many reliable Greek manuscripts do not have this verse, and it is missing in many modern translations. See Ezekiel 34:16.

f 18:13 The Aramaic is "the ninety-nine that did not go astray."

g 18:14 As translated from the Aramaic figure of speech. The Greek is "little ones."

h 18:14 Implied in the context.

i 18:15 Although the words "against you," are not found in the most reliable Greek manuscripts, they are included in the Hebrew Matthew and Aramaic, along with a number of Greek texts. The Hebrew Matthew indicates that Jesus addressed these words to Peter directly: "At that time Jesus said to Simon, called Keefa..."

j 18:15 See Leviticus 19:17.

one or two others with you. You'll be fulfilling what the Scripture teaches when it says, 'Every word may be verified by the testimony of two or three witnesses.'[a] [17]And if he refuses to listen, then share the issue with the entire church in hopes of restoration.[b] If he still refuses to respond, disregarding the fellowship of his church family, you must disregard him as though he were an outsider, on the same level as an unrepentant sinner."[c]

[18]Receive this truth: Whatever you forbid on earth will be considered to be forbidden in heaven,[d] and whatever you release on earth will be considered to be released in heaven. [19]Again, I give you an eternal truth: If two of you agree to ask God for something in a symphony of prayer,[e] my heavenly Father will do it for you. [20]For wherever two or three come together in honor of my name,[f] I am right there with them!"

Unlimited Forgiveness

[21]Later Peter approached Jesus and said, "How many times do I have to forgive my fellow believer who keeps offending me? Seven times?"[g]

[22]Jesus answered, **"Not seven times, Peter, but seventy times seven times!**[h] [23]The lessons of forgiveness in heaven's kingdom realm can be illustrated like this:

"There once was a king who had servants who had borrowed money from the royal treasury. He decided to settle accounts with each of them. [24]As he began the process, it came to his attention that one of his servants[i]

---

a 18:16 See Deuteronomy 19:16.
b 18:17 Implied throughout the context.
c 18:17 Or "a pagan or a tax collector." Again, this is in hope of ultimate restoration. For even pagans and tax collectors can be saved. God is able to turn the wandering one back, as Jesus taught in the parable of the lost lamb (see vv. 11–14).
d 18:18 Or "Whatever you bind (Aramaic 'harness') on earth will have been bound in heaven." See Matthew 16:19 with accompanying footnote.
e 18:19 The Greek word used here is *sumphoneo,* from which we get our English word "symphony." The Aramaic is "if you are deserving of what you pray for." The implication is that God will not give you what you are not yet ready for, just as an earthly father would not give his eight-year-old a car to drive.
f 18:20 Or "in my name."
g 18:21 The Hebrew Matthew is "Seven times in one day?"
h 18:22 Or "seventy-seven times." This is a metaphor for an attitude of forgiveness that is limitless.
i 18:24 Although the Greek uses the word for "servant," it means someone who ruled under the king, perhaps one of his magistrates or cabinet members who had authority over finances.

owed him one billion dollars.[a] So he summoned the servant before him and said to him, 'Pay me what you owe me.' [25]When his servant was unable to repay his debt, the king ordered that he be sold as a slave along with his wife and children and every possession they owned as payment toward his debt. [26]The servant threw himself facedown at his master's feet and begged for mercy. 'Please be patient with me. Just give me more time and I will repay you all that I owe.' [27]Upon hearing his pleas, the king had compassion on his servant, and released him, and forgave his entire debt.

[28]"No sooner had the servant left when he met one of his fellow servants, who owed him twenty thousand dollars[b] He seized him by the throat and began to choke him, saying, 'You'd better pay me right now everything you owe me!' [29]His fellow servant threw himself facedown at his feet and begged, 'Please be patient with me. If you'll just give me time, I will repay you all that is owed.' [30]But the one who had his debt forgiven stubbornly refused to forgive what was owed him. He had his fellow servant thrown into prison and demanded he remain there until he repaid the debt in full.

[31]"When his associates saw what was going on, they were outraged and went to the king and told him the whole story. [32]The king said to him, 'You scoundrel![c] Is this the way you respond to my mercy? Because you begged me, I forgave you the massive debt that you owed me. [33]Why didn't you show the same mercy to your fellow servant that I showed to you?' [34]In a fury of anger, the king turned him over to the prison guards to be tortured until all his debt was repaid. [35]In this same way, my heavenly Father will deal with any of you if you do not release forgiveness from your heart[d] toward your fellow believer."

---

a 18:24 Or "ten thousand talents," an unbelievable amount of money. A talent could be compared to the wages earned over decades. The number ten thousand is a Hebrew metaphor for "myriad." The point is, the servant owed a huge amount of money that he was simply unable to repay.
b 18:28 Or "one hundred silver coins." This would be a denarii, which is about a day's wages. So the servant owed his friend about three months' wages.
c 18:32 The Hebrew Matthew is "You servant of Belial!"
d 18:35 The Hebrew Matthew is "with a perfect heart."

Nineteen

Questions about Divorce

[1]After Jesus finished teaching them, he left Galilee and made his way toward the district of Judea, east of the Jordan River. [2]Massive crowds followed him and he healed all who were sick.[a] [3]The "separated ones" were intent on putting Jesus to the test with difficult questions, so they approached him and asked, "Is it lawful for a man to divorce his wife for any reason?"[b]

[4]**"Haven't you read the Scriptures about creation?"** Jesus replied. **"The Creator made us male and female from the very beginning,**[c] **[5]and 'For this reason a man will leave his father and mother and live with his wife.**[d] **And the two will become one flesh.'**[e] **[6]From then on, they are no longer two, but united as one. So what God unites let no one divide!"**

[7]They responded, "So then why did Moses command us to give a certificate of divorce and it would be lawful?"

[8]Jesus said, **"Moses permitted you to divorce because your hearts are so hard and stubborn,**[f] **but originally there was no such thing. [9]But I**

---

a 19:2 As translated from the Hebrew Matthew.

b 19:3 This a clever test by the Pharisees. Jesus was now in Judea and under the jurisdiction of Herod Antipas, the one who had John beheaded over challenging his divorce. They were hoping Jesus would say something that could get him arrested and killed by Herod. Their question was based on Deuteronomy 24:1. Jewish divorce law had a "for any reason" clause that made divorce legal. They were pressing Jesus for his interpretation of this "for any reason" law.

c 19:4 See Genesis 1:27 and 5:2. Notice that Jesus highlights gender difference in the context of marriage.

d 19:5 Or "cling to his wife."

e 19:5 See Genesis 2:24.

f 19:8 That is, in a fallen world with frail human beings, God allowed divorce to accommodate broken humanity. Jesus restates divorce as being permitted only in the case of immorality. Adultery breaks the bond of marriage and requires God's healing grace. Those testing Jesus were attempting to trap him by getting him to say something against Moses, their venerated historical leader.

say to you, whoever leaves his wife for any reason other than immorality, then takes another wife is living in adultery. And whoever takes a divorced woman in marriage is also living in adultery."[a]

[10]His disciples spoke up and said, "If this is the standard, then it seems better to never get married."

[11]**"Not everyone is meant to remain single—only those whom God gives grace to be unmarried.**[b] [12]**For some are born to celibacy; others have been made eunuchs by others. And there are some who have chosen to live in celibacy for the sacred purpose of heaven's kingdom realm.**[c] [13]**Let those who can, accept this truth for themselves.**

Jesus and Little Children

[13]Then they brought little children to Jesus so that he would lay his hands on them, bless them, and pray for them.[d] But the disciples scolded those who brought the children, saying, "Don't bother him with this now!"

[14]Jesus overheard them and said, **"I want little children to come to me, so never interfere with them when they want to come, for heaven's kingdom realm is composed of beloved ones**[e] **like these! Listen to this truth: no**

---

a 19:9 As translated from the Hebrew Matthew, Aramaic, and some Greek manuscripts. The majority of Greek manuscripts do not include the last sentence.

b 19:11 Or "This doesn't apply to everyone, but only to those to whom it (grace for singleness) has been given."

c 19:12 Three types of "celibates" are mentioned. 1) those who from birth have grace to remain celibate. 2) a male who has been castrated, usually before puberty, which would greatly affect the hormonal changes of a boy becoming an adult. In biblical times, these eunuchs were chosen to be male servants of a king, having been castrated in order to ensure they don't have sex with the king's harem. 3) a metaphorical class of people (male and female) who are like "spiritual eunuchs," having been chosen to never use the bride of Christ for their own purposes. Jesus gives us a parable of God's servants who will lead the church but never harm or use the bride of Christ for their own desires. They will always point the bride to her Bridegroom, Jesus Christ. They have made themselves "eunuchs" and are determined to extend God's kingdom, not their own. The rare Greek verb for "make themselves eunuchs" can also refer to being "always watchful, sleepless, diligent." To become a "spiritual eunuch" has nothing to do with sex, but with always watching out for the interests of our King, and not taking for ourselves what only belongs to him in order to serve our own desires.

d 19:13 See Genesis 48:14.

e 19:14 As translated from the Aramaic, which uses the word for "beloved," found only twice in the New Testament. The Greek is "little children." God receives little children into his kingdom.

one will enter the kingdom realm of heaven unless he becomes like one of these!"[a] [15]Then he laid his hands on each of them and went on his way.

A Rich Young Man Questions Jesus

[16]Then a teenager[b] approached Jesus and bowed before him,[c] saying, "Wonderful teacher[d]—is there a good work I have to do to obtain eternal life?"

[17]Jesus answered, **"Why would you call me wonderful? God alone is wonderful.[e] And why would you ask what good work you need to do? Keep the commandments and you'll enter into the life of God."**

[18]"Which ones?" he asked.

Jesus said, **"Don't murder, don't commit adultery, don't steal, don't lie, [19]honor your father and mother, and love those around you as you love yourself."[f]**

[20]"But I've always obeyed every one of them without fail," the young man replied. "What else do I lack?"

[21]Jesus said to him, **"If you really want to be perfect,[g] go immediately and sell everything you own. Give all your money to the poor and your treasure will be transferred into heaven. Then come back and follow me for the rest of your life."**

[22]When the young man heard these words, he walked away angry,[h] for he was extremely wealthy.

[23]Then Jesus turned to his disciples and said, "Listen. Do you understand

---

a 19:14 As translated from the Hebrew Matthew. This last sentence is missing in the Greek text.
b 19:16 This is supplied from verse 22. The Aramaic uses a word that identifies his age as a teenager.
c 19:16 As translated from the Hebrew Matthew. This is missing from the Majority Greek text.
d 19:16 As translated from the Aramaic, which uses the word *tawa*, meaning "wonderful, good, gifted." Some Greek manuscripts have only "teacher (rabbi)."
e 19:17 At least one of the earliest Greek manuscripts reads "There is no one good but my Father in the heavens."
f 19:19 See Exodus 20:12–17 and Leviticus 19:18. Notice that Jesus left out the commandment "Don't covet." He addresses this with the young man in verse 21 and exposes the need to abandon all to follow Jesus.
g 19:21 Or "fully developed morally, mature."
h 19:22 As translated from the Hebrew Matthew. The Greek reads "grieved, sorrowful."

how difficult it is for the rich to enter into heaven's kingdom realm? [24]In fact, it's easier to stuff a heavy rope[a] through the eye of a needle than it is for the wealthy to enter into God's kingdom realm!"

[25]Stunned and bewildered, his disciples asked, "Then who in the world can possibly be saved?"

[26]Looking straight into their eyes, Jesus replied, **"Humanly speaking, no one, because no one can save himself.[b] But what seems impossible to you is never impossible to God!"**

[27]Then Peter blurted out, "Here we are. We've given up everything to follow you. What reward will there be for us?"

[28]Jesus responded, **"Listen to the truth: In the age of the restoration of all things,[c] when the Son of Man sits on his glorious throne, you who have followed me will have twelve thrones of your own, and you will govern[d] the twelve tribes of Israel. [29]For anyone who has left behind their home and property,[e] leaving family—brothers or sisters, mothers or fathers,[f] or children—for my sake, they will be repaid a hundred times over and will inherit eternal life. [30]But many who push themselves to be first will find themselves last. And those who are willing to be last will find themselves to be first."[g]**

---

a 19:24 As translated from the Aramaic. The Greek is "to stuff a camel through the eye of a needle." The Aramaic word for both "rope" and "camel" is the homonym *gamla*. This could be an instance of the Aramaic text being misread by the Greek translators as "camel" instead of "rope." Regardless, this becomes a metaphor for something impossible. It would be like saying, "It's as hard as making pigs fly!" See also Luke 18:25.

b 19:26 Implied in the text.

c 19:28 Or "in the second birth" (Hebrew Matthew) or "in the new realm" (Aramaic). The Greek word *palingenesia* is only used one other time in the New Testament (Titus 3:5) and refers to our rebirth. See also 2 Corinthians 5:17, Acts 3:21, and Revelation 3:21.

d 19:28 Or "judge."

e 19:29 Or "fields."

f 19:29 The Aramaic and a few Greek manuscripts include "or wife." The majority of reliable Greek manuscripts do not include it.

g 19:30 Or "Many of the first ones will be last and many of the last ones will be first."

Twenty

A Parable of Workers in the Vineyard

¹"This will help you understand the way heaven's kingdom operates:

"There once was a wealthy landowner who went out at daybreak to hire all the laborers he could find to work in his vineyard. ²After agreeing to pay them the standard day's wage, he put them to work. ³Then at nine o'clock, as he was passing through the town square, he found others standing around without work. ⁴He told them, 'Come and work for me in my vineyard and I'll pay you a fair wage.' ⁵So off they went to join the others. He did the same thing at noon and again at three o'clock, making the same arrangement as he did with the others.

⁶"Hoping to finish his harvest that day, he went to the town square again at five o'clock[a] and found more who were idle. So he said to them, 'Why have you been here all day without work?'

⁷"'Because no one hired us,' they answered.

"So he said to them, 'Then go and join my crew and work in my vineyard.'

⁸"When evening came, the owner of the vineyard went to his foreman and said, 'Call in all the laborers, line them up, and pay them the same wages, starting with the most recent ones I hired and finishing with the ones who worked all day.'

⁹"When those hired late in the day came to be paid, they were given a full day's wage. ¹⁰And when those who had been hired first came to be

---

a 20:6 Or "in the eleventh hour (about five o'clock)."

paid, they were convinced that they would receive more. But everyone was paid the standard wage. ¹¹When they realized what had happened, they were offended and complained to the landowner, saying, ¹²'You're treating us unfairly! They've only worked for one hour while we've slaved and sweated all day under the scorching sun. You've made them equal to us!'

¹³"The landowner replied, 'Friends, I'm not being unfair—I'm doing exactly what I said. Didn't you agree to work for the standard wage? ¹⁴If I want to give those who only worked for an hour equal pay, what does that matter to you? ¹⁵Don't I have the right to do what I want with what is mine? Why should my generosity make you jealous of them?'[a]

¹⁶"Now you can understand what I meant when I said[b] that the first will end up last and the last will end up being first. Everyone is invited, but few are the chosen.'"[c]

Jesus Again Prophesies of His Death

¹⁷Jesus was about to go to Jerusalem, so he took his twelve disciples aside privately and said to them, ¹⁸**"Listen to me. We're on our way to Jerusalem, and I need to remind you that the Son of Man will be handed over to the religious leaders and scholars, and they will sentence him to be executed. ¹⁹And they will hand him over to the Romans[d] to be mocked, tortured, and crucified. Yet three days later he will be raised to life again."**

The Ambition of James and John

²⁰The wife of Zebedee approached Jesus with her sons, James and John. She knelt before him and asked him for a favor.

²¹He said to her, **"What is it that you want?"**

a 20:15 Or "Is your eye evil because I am good?"
b 20:16 Implied in the context of the parable, which illustrates Jesus' words in 19:30.
c 20:16 As translated from the Hebrew Matthew, Aramaic, and a few later Greek manuscripts. This logion is not included in the majority of the Greek manuscripts but is found in Matthew 22:14.
d 20:19 Or "Gentiles." By implication, the Romans.

She answered, "Make the decree[a] that these, my sons, will rule with you in your kingdom—one sitting on your right hand, one on your left."

²²Jesus replied, **"You don't know what you are asking."** Then, looking in the eyes of James and John, Jesus said, **"Are you prepared to drink from the cup of suffering that I am about to drink? And are you able to endure the baptism into death that I am about to endure?"**[b]

They answered him, "Yes, we are able."[c]

²³**"You will indeed drink the cup of my suffering and be immersed into my death,"**[d] Jesus told them. **"But to be the ones who sit at the place of highest honor is not mine to decide. My Father is the one who chooses them and prepares them."**

²⁴The other ten disciples were listening to all of this, and a jealous anger arose among them against the two brothers. ²⁵Jesus, knowing their thoughts, called them to his side and said, **"Kings and those with great authority in this world rule oppressively over their subjects, like tyrants. ²⁶But this is not your calling. You will lead by a completely different model. The greatest one among you will live as the one who is called to serve others, ²⁷because the greatest honor and authority is reserved for the one with the heart of a servant. ²⁸For even the Son of Man did not come expecting to be served by everyone, but to serve everyone, and to give his life in exchange for the salvation of many."**[e]

---

a 20:21 Or "Give the order."
b 20:22 Or "Are you able to drink from the cup I am about to drink?"
c 20:22 The naïveté of James and John is glaring. Their ambition is emphasized by having their mother come to ask this favor. This event is included immediately after Jesus prophesied for the third time his coming crucifixion. Their hearts were set on their own advancement rather than intercession for their Master.
d 20:23 As translated from the Aramaic and the Hebrew Matthew.
e 20:28 As translated from the Aramaic. The Greek is "a ransom paid for many."

Two Blind Men Healed

²⁹As Jesus approached[a] Jericho an immense crowd gathered and followed him. ³⁰And there were two blind men sitting on the roadside. When they heard that it was Jesus passing by, they shouted, "Son of David,[b] show us mercy, Lord!" ³¹Those in the crowd scolded them and told them to be quiet. But the blind men screamed out even louder, "Jesus, Son of David, show us mercy, Lord!"

³²So Jesus stopped and had them brought to him. He asked them, **"What do you want me to do for you?"**

³³They said, "Lord, we want to see! Heal us!"

³⁴Jesus was deeply moved with compassion[c] toward them. So he touched their eyes, and instantly they could see! Jesus said to them, **"Your faith has healed you."** And all the people praised God because of this miracle.[d] And the two men became his followers from that day onward.

---

a 20:29 As translated from the Hebrew Matthew. The Greek is "As Jesus left Jericho." See also Luke 18:35–43, which may indicate that Luke used the Hebrew Matthew as one of his sources.
b 20:30 The term "Son of David" was used for the Messiah. The blind men believed Jesus was the Messiah.
c 20:34 The Aramaic is "Jesus had nurturing love toward them."
d 20:34 This and the previous sentence, "Your faith has healed you," are translated from the Hebrew Matthew. They are missing from the Greek text.

Twenty-one

Jesus' Triumphal Entry into Jerusalem

[1]Now, as they were approaching Jerusalem they arrived at the place of the stables[a] near the Mount of Olives. Jesus sent two of his disciples ahead, saying, [2]**"As soon as you enter the village, you will find a donkey tethered along with her young colt. Untie them both and bring them to me. [3]And if anyone stops you and asks, 'What are you doing?' just tell them, 'The Lord of All needs them,' and he will let you take them."**

[4]All of this happened to fulfill the prophecy:

> [5]**Tell Zion's daughter: "Look, your King arrives!**
> **He's coming to you full of gentleness,**
> **Sitting on a donkey, riding on a donkey's colt."**[b]

[6]So the two disciples went on ahead and did as Jesus had instructed them. [7]They brought the donkey and her colt to him and placed their cloaks and prayer shawls on the colt, and Jesus rode on it.

[8]Then an exceptionally large crowd gathered and carpeted the road before him with their cloaks and prayer shawls.[c] Others cut down branches from trees to spread in his path. [9]Jesus rode in the center of the procession—crowds going before him and crowds coming behind him, and they all

---

a 21:1 Or "Bethphage," which in Aramaic means "the house of stables." Transliterated into Greek it means "the house of unripe figs."

b 21:5 See Zechariah 9:9. Kings rode on horses, not donkeys. He chose the young colt as a symbol of humility and gentleness.

c 21:8 See 2 Kings 9:13.

shouted, "Bring the victory, Lord,[a] Son of David! He comes with the blessings of being sent from the Lord Yahweh![b] We celebrate with praises to God in the highest!"

¹⁰As Jesus entered Jerusalem, the people went wild with excitement—the entire city was thrown into an uproar![c] ¹¹Some asked, "Who is this man?" And the crowds shouted back, "This is Jesus! He's the prophet from Nazareth[d] of Galilee!"

Jesus in the Temple

¹²Upon entering Jerusalem Jesus went directly into the temple area and drove away all the merchants who were buying and selling their goods. He overturned the tables of the money changers and the stands of those selling doves.[e] ¹³And he said to them, **"My dwelling place will be known as a house of prayer, but you have made it into a hangout for thieves!"**[f]

¹⁴Then the blind and the crippled came into the temple courts, and Jesus healed them all. And the children circled around him shouting out, "Blessings and praises to the Son of David!"

¹⁵But when the chief priests and religious scholars heard the children shouting and saw all the wonderful miracles of healing, they were furious.[g] ¹⁶They said to Jesus, "Don't you hear what these children are saying? This is not right!"

---

a 21:9 Or "Hosanna," an Aramaic word that means "O, save (bring the victory), Lord!" The crowds were recognizing Jesus as Yahweh's Messiah. By shouting out, "Son of David," they were clearly expecting Jesus to immediately overthrow the Roman oppression and set the nation free. Many want victory before the cross, but true victory comes after resurrection!

b 21:9 As translated from the Aramaic. See Psalm 118:25–26.

c 21:10 Or "The city was shaken (like with an earthquake)!"

d 21:11 The Hebrew word Nazara (Nazareth) can be translated "Branch" or "Victorious One." They were shouting, "This is Jesus, the Victorious One of Galilee!"

e 21:12 The revered theologian and historian Jerome (son of Eusebius) was the translator of the Bible into Latin. He also wrote a commentary on Matthew, which includes a fascinating thought about Jesus overturning the tables. Jerome writes, "For a certain fiery and starry light shone from his eyes, and the majesty of God gleamed in his face."

f 21:13 See Isaiah 56:5–7 and Jeremiah 7:11.

g 21:15 The Aramaic is "It seemed evil to them."

Jesus answered, **"Yes, I hear them. But have you never heard the words 'You have fashioned the lips of children and toddlers to compose your praises'?"**[h]

[17] Jesus then left at once for the nearby village of Bethany, where he spent the night.[i]

[18] While walking back into the city the next morning, he got hungry. [19] He noticed a lone fig tree by the side of the path and walked over to see if there was any fruit on it, but there was none—he found only leaves. So he spoke to the fig tree and said, **"You will be barren and will never bear fruit again!"** Instantly the fig tree[j] shriveled up right in front of their eyes!

[20] Astonished, his disciples asked, "How did you make this fig tree instantly wither and die?"

[21] Jesus replied, **"Listen to the truth. If you have no doubt of God's power and speak out of faith's fullness, you can be the ones who speak to a tree and it will wither away. Even more than that, you could say to this mountain, 'Be lifted up and be thrown into the sea' and it will be done.**[k] [22] **Everything you pray for with the fullness of faith you will receive!"**[l]

The Authority of Jesus

[23] After this Jesus went into the temple courts and taught the people. The leading priests and Jewish elders approached him and interrupted him and

---

h 21:16 See Psalm 8:2. The Greek text quoting from Psalm 8 does not agree with either the Hebrew text, the Septuagint, or the Aramaic, but seems to line up with a version found in the Dead Sea Scrolls. You might say Jesus paraphrased the Scriptures to speak to his generation.

i 21:17 The Hebrew Matthew adds, "There he was explaining the kingdom of God."

j 21:19 The fig tree is first mentioned in Genesis 3:7, with its leaves being a "covering" for fallen Adam and Eve to hide behind. It is connected to the Tree of Knowledge of Good and Evil, and became a hiding place for Zacchaeus, who climbed a sycamore-fig tree to see Jesus. Many also equate the fig tree as being a symbol of Israel.

k 21:21 The mountain and the sea are both metaphors. Mountains speak of kingdoms, and the sea represents the nations (e.g., "sea of humanity"). Faith brings the reality of the kingdom realm into the nations.

l 21:22 Jesus taught his disciples that if faith's fullness lived in them, they could speak to the physical creation around them and it would respond. Faith unlocks great authority for the believer.

asked, "By what power[a] do you do these things, and who granted you the authority to teach here?"

[24]Jesus answered them, **"I too have a question to ask you. If you can answer this question, then I will tell you by what power I do these things. [25]From where did John's authority to baptize come from? From heaven or from people?"**

[26]They stepped away and debated among themselves, saying, "How should we answer this? If we say from heaven, he will say to us, 'Then why didn't you respond to John and believe what he said?' But if we deny that God gave him his authority, we'll be mobbed by the people, for they're convinced that John was God's prophet."

[27]So they finally answered, "We don't know."

"Then neither will I tell you from where my power comes to do these things!" he replied.

The Parable of Two Sons

[28]Jesus said to his critics,[b] **"Tell me what you think of this parable:**

"There once was a man with two sons. The father came to the first and said, 'Son, I want you to go and work in the vineyard today.' [29]The son replied, 'I'd rather not.' But afterward, he deeply regretted what he said to his father, changed his mind, and decided to go to the vineyard. [30]The father approached the second son and said the same thing to him. The son replied, 'Father, I will go and do as you said.' But he never did—he didn't go to the vineyard. [31]Tell me now, which of these two sons did the will of his father?"

They answered him, "The first one."

Jesus said, **"You're right. For many sinners, tax collectors, and prostitutes are going into God's kingdom realm ahead of you! [32]John came to**

---

a 21:23 As translated from the Hebrew Matthew. The Greek is "authority." See also verses 24 and 27.
b 21:28 As translated from the Hebrew Matthew.

show you the path of goodness and righteousness,[a] yet the despised and outcasts believed in him, but you did not. When you saw them turn, you neither repented of your ways nor believed his words."

The Parable of the Rejected Son

[33]"Pay close attention to this parable," Jesus said. "There once was an honorable man who planted a vineyard.[b] He built a fence around it,[c] dug out a pit for pressing the grapes, and erected a watchtower. Afterward he leased the land to tenant farmers and then went a distance away. [34]At harvest time he sent his servants to the tenants to collect the portion that was due him as the lord of the vineyard. [35]But the tenants seized his servants and beat one, killed another, and stoned another.[d] [36]So the landowner sent other servants, even more than at first, but they were mistreated the same way. [37]Finally, he sent his own son to them, and he said to himself, 'Perhaps with my own son standing before them they will be ashamed of what they've done.'[e] [38]But when the tenants saw the son, they said, 'This is the heir! Let's kill him and then we can have his inheritance!' [39]So they violently seized him, took him outside the vineyard, and murdered him.

[40]"You tell me, when the lord of the vineyard comes, what do you think he will do to those tenants?"

[41]They answered, "He will bring a horrible death to those who did this evil and he will completely destroy them. Then he'll lease his vineyard to different tenants who will be faithful to give him the portion he deserves."

[42]Jesus said to them, **"Haven't you ever read the Scripture that says:**

---

a 21:32 Or "the way of righteousness (justice)." The Aramaic is "the way of goodness." The translation includes both concepts.

b 21:33 As translated from the Hebrew Matthew. The Greek is "landowner." See Isaiah 5:1–7.

c 21:33 The Aramaic can be translated "He planted a vineyard by a stream."

d 21:35 The obvious meaning of the parable is this: God is the landowner, the servants he sends are God's prophets, and the son is Jesus Christ.

e 21:37 As translated from the Aramaic. The Greek is "They will respect my son."

The very stone the builder rejected as flawed
Has now become the most important
Capstone of the arch.
This was the Lord's plan[a]—
Isn't it a miracle for our eyes to behold?[b]

[43]"This is why I say to you that the kingdom realm of God will be taken from you and given to a people[c] who will be bear its fruit. [44]The one who comes against this stone[d] will be broken, but the one on whom it falls will be pulverized!"[e]

[45]When the leading priests and the "separated ones" realized that the parable was referring to them, they were [46]outraged and wanted to arrest him at once. But they were afraid of the reaction of the crowds, because the people considered him to be a prophet.

a   21:42 The Aramaic and the Hebrew Matthew read, "This came from the presence of (next to) Lord Yahweh and is a marvel in our eyes."
b   21:42 See Psalm 118:22–23. The words "capstone of the arch" could also be translated "cornerstone" or "keystone." This is an obvious metaphor of Jesus Christ. He is a Stone that many will stumble over, and a Stone that will fall upon the unbeliever.
c   21:43 Or "nation." The Hebrew Matthew and Aramaic can be translated "Gentiles." This is a prophecy of the church being given access to the kingdom of God through faith in Jesus Christ.
d   21:44 Or "falls upon this stone." Some manuscripts do not include verse 44. The Hebrew Matthew does not have the last clause of verse 44.
e   21:44 See Isaiah 8:14–15 and Daniel 2:34–35.

Twenty-two

Parable of the Wedding Feast

[1]As was his custom, Jesus continued to teach the people by using allegories. [2]He illustrated the reality of heaven's kingdom realm by saying, **"There once was a king who arranged an extravagant wedding feast for his son.**[a] **[3]On the day the festivities were set to begin, he sent his servants**[b] **to summon all the invited guests, but they chose not to come. [4]So the king sent even more servants to inform the invited guests, saying, 'Come, for the sumptuous feast is now ready! The oxen and fattened cattle have been killed and everything is prepared, so come! Come to the wedding feast for my son and his bride!'**

[5]**"But the invited guests were not impressed. One was preoccupied with his business; another went off to his farming enterprise. [6]And the rest seized the king's messengers and shamefully mistreated them, and even killed them. [7]This infuriated the king! So he sent his soldiers to execute those murderers and had their city burned to the ground.**[c]

[8]**"Then the king said to his servants, 'The wedding feast is ready, yet those who had been invited to attend didn't deserve the honor. [9]Now I want you to go into the streets and alleyways**[d] **and invite anyone and everyone you find to come and enjoy the wedding feast in honor of my son.'**

a 22:2 See Isaiah 25:6–8.
b 22:3 God is the king who prepares his kingdom feast for his Son, Jesus Christ. The messenger-servants are the prophets he sends to summon the people to enter into the love feast of Jesus. It is all about the wedding of the Lamb to the bride of Christ. What a glorious feast is prepared for us!
c 22:7 This was fulfilled by the Roman prince Titus (who eventually became emperor of Rome) in the Roman war of AD 67–70.
d 22:9 The Aramaic is "Go to the ends of the roads."

[10]"So the servants went out into the city streets and invited everyone to come to the wedding feast, good and bad alike, until the banquet hall was crammed with people! [11]Now, when the king entered the banquet hall, he looked with glee over all his guests. But then he noticed a guest who was not wearing the wedding robe provided for him.[a] [12]So he said, 'My friend, how is it that you're here and you're not wearing your wedding garment?' But the man was speechless.

[13]"Then the king turned to his servants and said, 'Tie him up and throw him into the outer darkness,[b] where there will be great sorrow, with weeping and grinding of teeth.' [14]For everyone is invited[c] to enter in, but few respond in excellence.'"[d]

The "Separated Ones" Try to Entrap Jesus

[15]Then the "separated ones" came together to make a plan to entrap Jesus with his own words. [16]So they sent some of their disciples together with some staunch supporters of Herod.[e] They said to Jesus, "Teacher, we know that you're an honest man of integrity and you teach us the truth of God's ways. We can clearly see that you're not one who speaks only to win the people's favor, because you speak the truth without regard to the consequences.[f] [17]So tell us, then, what you think. Is it proper for us Jews to pay taxes to Caesar or not?"

---

a 22:11 Implied in the text. Those invited to come from the streets had no opportunity to buy wedding clothes. This wedding robe is a picture of the garment of righteousness that grace provides for us. The man without the wedding garment had one provided, but he didn't want to change into new clothes. A change is necessary, for our King provides garments of white linen for us to wear, our wedding garments. See Isaiah 52:1 and Revelation 19:8.

b 22:13 The Hebrew Matthew is "the lowest hell (sheol)."

c 22:14 Or "Many are called." This can be understood to be a Semitic figure of speech that universalizes the invitation. See also Matthew 20:28.

d 22:14 The Greek word eklektoi can mean "chosen," but it can also be translated "worthy, pure, choice, excellent." See 2 John 1, 13.

e 22:16 The Hebrew Matthew is "They took violent men from Herod." The Aramaic is "They took men from Herod's household." By bringing with them loyalists to Rome (Herodians), the "separated ones" were convinced that Jesus would offend either the Jews, who despised paying the "poll tax" required of every adult male, or those political followers of Herod who sided with the Roman occupation.

f 22:16 Or "You don't look into the faces of men (before you speak the truth)."

¹⁸Jesus knew the malice that was hidden behind their cunning ploy and said, **"Why are you testing me, you imposters who think you have all the answers? ¹⁹Show me one of the Roman coins."** So they brought him a silver coin used to pay the tax. ²⁰**"Now, tell me, whose head is on this coin and whose inscription is stamped on it?"**

²¹"Caesar's," they replied.

Jesus said, **"Precisely, for the coin bears the image of the emperor Caesar.**[a] **Well, then, you should pay the emperor what is due to the emperor. But because you bear the image of God,**[b] **give back to God all that belongs to him."**

²²The imposters were baffled in the presence of all the people and were unable to trap Jesus with his words. So they left, stunned by Jesus' words.

Marriage and the Resurrection

²³Some of the Sadducees, a religious group that denied there was a resurrection of the dead,[c] came to ask Jesus this question: ²⁴"Teacher, the law of Moses teaches that if a man dies before he has children, his brother should marry the widow and raise up children for his brother's family line.[d] ²⁵Now, there was a family with seven brothers. The oldest got married but soon died, leaving his widow for his brother. ²⁶The second brother married and also died, and the third also. This was repeated down to the seventh brother, ²⁷when finally the woman also died. So here's our dilemma: ²⁸which of the seven brothers will be the woman's husband when she's resurrected from the dead, since they all were once married to her?"

²⁹Jesus answered them, **"You are deluded, because your hearts are not filled with the revelation of the Scriptures or the power of God. ³⁰For after**

---

a 22:21 Actual coins from that era have been found with the emperor's image and a superscription saying, "Tiberius Caesar Augustus, son of the divine Augustus."

b 22:21 Implied in the text. The coin belongs to Caesar because it carries his image. We have an obligation to God because we carry his image.

c 22:23 The Aramaic clearly states that the Sadducees said to Jesus, "There is no life after death."

d 22:24 See Deuteronomy 25:5–10.

the resurrection, men and women will not marry, just like the angels of heaven don't marry. [31]Haven't you read what God said: [32]'I am the Living God,[a] the God of Abraham, the God of Isaac, and the God of Jacob'? God is not the God of the dead, but of the living."[b]

[33]When the crowds heard this they were dazed, stunned over such wisdom![c]

The Greatest Commandment

[34]When the "separated ones" heard that Jesus had silenced the Sadducees, they called a meeting to discuss how to trap Jesus. [35]Then one of them, a religious scholar, posed this question to test him: [36]"Teacher, which commandment in the law is the greatest?"

[37]Jesus answered him, "'Love[d] the Lord your God with every passion of your heart, with all the energy of your being, and with every thought that is within you.'[e] [38]This is the great and supreme commandment. [39]And the second is like it in importance: 'You must love your friend[f] in the same way you love yourself.'[g] [40]Contained within these commandments to love you will find all the meaning of the Law and the Prophets."

Jesus, Son of David—Lord of David

[41]While all the "separated ones" were gathered together, Jesus took the opportunity to pose a question of his own: [42]"What do you think about the Anointed One? Whose son is he?"

---

a 22:32 As translated from the Aramaic and implied in the Greek.

b 22:32 The implication Jesus is making is that Abraham, Isaac, and Jacob were all alive (in glory) when God spoke to Moses in the burning bush. See Exodus 3:6.

c 22:33 As translated from the Hebrew Matthew. The Greek is "teaching."

d 22:37 The Hebrew Matthew is "worship," also quoted as "worship" by Justin Martyr (ca. AD 165), *First Apology* XXI.

e 22:37 Or "with all your mind." See Deuteronomy 6:5.

f 22:39 As translated from the Aramaic word *kareb*, which means "one who is close to you (emotionally or by proximity)." The Greek is "neighbor."

g 22:39 See Leviticus 19:18.

"The son of David," they replied.

⁴³Then Jesus said to them, **"How is it that David, inspired by the Holy Spirit, could call his son the Lord? For didn't he say:**

> ⁴⁴**The Lord Jehovah said to my Lord,**
> **"Sit near me in the place of authority**
> **Until I subdue all your enemies under Your feet"?**ᵃ

⁴⁵**"So how could David call his own son 'the Lord Jehovah'?"**ᵇ

⁴⁶No one could come up with an answer. And from that day on none of the "separated ones" had the courage to question Jesus any longer.

---

a 22:44 See Psalm 110:1, which is the Old Testament passage of Scripture most often quoted in the New Testament.

b 22:45 As translated from the Aramaic. To those who insisted on only interpreting the Scriptures literally, Jesus was proving there was a deeper spiritual interpretation. To say the Messiah would be the Son of David means that the Anointed One would manifest the qualities and devotion that David walked in. A true "spiritual" son of David.

Twenty-three

Superficial Spirituality versus Genuine Humility

¹Then Jesus addressed both the crowds and his disciples and said, ²**"The religious scholars and the 'separated ones' sit on Moses's throne**[a] **as the authorized interpreters of the Law.** ³So listen and follow what they teach, but don't do what they do, for they tell you one thing and do another. ⁴They tie on your backs an oppressive burden of religious obligations and insist that you carry it, but will never lift a finger to help ease your load. ⁵Everything they do is done for show and to be noticed by others. They want to be seen as "holy,"[b] so they wear oversized prayer boxes on their arms and foreheads with Scriptures inside, and wear extra-long tassels on their outer garments.[c] ⁶They crave the seats of highest honor at banquets and in their meeting places. ⁷And how they love to be admired by men with their titles of respect, aspiring to be recognized in public and have others call them 'Reverend.'[d]

⁸"But you are to be different from that. You are not to be called 'master,' for you have only one Master, and you are all brothers and sisters. ⁹And you are not to be addressed as 'father,'[e] for you have one Father, who is in heaven. ¹⁰Nor are you to be addressed as 'teacher,'[f] for you have

---

a 23:2 Moses's throne (Aramaic) was a special seat in the ancient synagogues where the most respected elders of the people would sit to instruct them.
b 23:5 Implied in the context.
c 23:5 See Numbers 15:38 and Deuteronomy 22:12.
d 23:7 Or "rabbi," an Aramaic word that means "master," "chief," "great one," or "teacher."
e 23:9 As translated from the Hebrew Matthew and the Aramaic. The Greek is "Call no one father."
f 23:10 Or "leader."

one Teacher, the Anointed One.[a] [11]The greatest among you will be the one who always serves others from the heart. [12]Remember this: If you have a lofty opinion of yourself and seek to be honored, you will be humbled. But if you have a modest opinion of yourself and choose to humble yourself, you will be honored."

Jesus Pronounces Seven Woes

[13]"Great sorrow awaits[b] you religious scholars and you 'separated ones'[c]—such frauds and pretenders! You do all you can to keep people from experiencing the reality of heaven's kingdom realm.[d] Not only do you refuse to enter in, you also forbid anyone else from entering in!

[14]"Great sorrow awaits you religious scholars and you 'separated ones'[e]—frauds and pretenders! For you eat up the widow's household with the ladle of your prayers. Because of this, you will receive a greater judgment.[f]

[15]"Great sorrow awaits you religious scholars and you 'separated ones'—such frauds and pretenders! For you will travel over lake and land to find one disciple, only to make him twice the child of hell[g] as yourselves.

[16]"You blind guides![h] Great sorrow awaits you, for you teach that there's nothing binding when you swear by God's temple, but if you swear by the gold of the temple, you are bound by your oath. [17]You are deceived

---

a 23:10 Jesus is emphasizing the priority of God over titles of men and over all teachers, fathers, and leaders. He is not teaching us to be disrespectful to teachers, fathers, and leaders, but that God must be in first place over all others. See Deuteronomy 17:9–10.

b 23:13 Or "woe."

c 23:13 Or "Pharisees," which means "separated ones." See also verses 14 and 15.

d 23:13 The Hebrew Matthew is "You have hidden the keys of knowledge and shut the kingdom of heaven from the children of men."

e 23:14 Or "Pharisees," which means "separated ones."

f 23:14 As translated from the Aramaic and the Hebrew Matthew. The most reliable Greek manuscripts do not include this verse, and it is omitted by modern translations.

g 23:15 Or "son of Gehenna." Gehenna is an Aramaic word for the garbage dump outside of Jerusalem, which became a metaphor for hell.

h 23:16 The Aramaic is "blind rescuers."

in your blindness![a] Which is greater, the gold or the temple that makes the gold sacred? [18]And you say that whoever takes an oath by swearing, 'By the altar,' it is nothing. But if you swear, 'By the gift upon the altar,' then you are obligated to keep your oath. [19]What deception! For what is greater, the gift or the altar that makes the gift sacred? [20]Whoever swears by the altar swears by the altar and everything offered on it. [21]And whoever swears by the temple swears by it and the one who dwells in it. [22]And whoever swears by heaven swears by the throne of God and by God, who sits upon it.

[23]"Great sorrow awaits you religious scholars and 'separated ones'[b]— frauds and pretenders! For you are obsessed with peripheral issues, like insisting on paying meticulous tithes on the smallest herbs that grow in your gardens.[c] These matters are fine, yet you ignore the most important duty of all: to walk in the love of God, to display mercy to others, and to live with integrity.[d] Readjust your values and place first things first. [24]What blind guides! Nitpickers! You will spoon out a gnat from your drink, yet at the same time you've gulped down a camel without realizing it![e]

[25]"Great sorrow awaits you religious scholars and 'separated ones'[f]— frauds and imposters! You are like one who will only wipe clean the outside of a cup or bowl, leaving the inside filthy. You are foolish to ignore the greed and self-indulgence that live like germs within you. [26]You are blind

---

a 23:17 Or "you blind fools."

b 23:23 Or "Pharisees," which means "separated ones."

c 23:23 Or "You tithe on mint, dill, and cumin (caraway seed)." See Leviticus 27:30, Numbers 18:12, and Deuteronomy 14:22–23. The law of Moses only obligated tithing on grain, wine, and oil. The religious scholars added to the law their interpretation, which added vegetables and herbs to their list of what should be tithed.

d 23:23 Or "faithfulness." The Hebrew Matthew is "justice, loving-kindness, and truth." The Aramaic is "justice, grace, and faith." See Micah 6:8 and Zechariah 7:9.

e 23:24 This is best seen as an Aramaic pun, because the Aramaic word for gnat is *qamla*, and the word for camel is *gamla*. The gnat becomes a metaphor of what is least and insignificant, for swallowing a gnat will not hurt you. But the camel becomes a picture of self-righteousness. To swallow a camel would indeed kill you!

f 23:25 Or "Pharisees," which means "separated ones."

and deaf[a] to your evil. Shouldn't the one who cleans the outside also be concerned with cleaning the inside? You need to have more than dishes; you need clean hearts!

[27]"Great sorrow awaits you religious scholars and 'separated ones'[b]— frauds and imposters! You are nothing more than tombs painted with fresh coats of white paint—tombs that look shining and beautiful on the outside, but within are found decaying corpses full of nothing but corruption. [28]Outwardly you masquerade as righteous people, but inside your hearts you are full of hypocrisy and lawlessness.

[29]"Great sorrow awaits you religious scholars and 'separated ones'[c]— frauds and imposters! You build memorials for the prophets your ancestors killed and decorate the monuments of the godly people your ancestors murdered. [30]Then you boast, 'If we had lived back then, we would never have permitted[d] them to kill the prophets.' [31]But your words and deeds testify that you are just like them and prove that you are indeed the descendants of those who murdered the prophets. [32]Go ahead and finish what your ancestors started! [33]You are nothing but snakes in the grass, the offspring of poisonous vipers! How will you escape the judgment of hell if you refuse to turn in repentance?[e]

[34]"For this reason I will send you more prophets and wise men and teachers of truth. Some you will crucify, and some you will beat mercilessly with whips in your meeting houses, abusing and persecuting them from city to city. [35]As your penalty, you will be held responsible for the righteous blood spilled and the murders of every godly person throughout your history—from the blood of righteous Abel to the blood of Zechariah, son of

---

a 23:26 As translated from the Aramaic.
b 23:27 Or "Pharisees," which means "separated ones."
c 23:29 Or "Pharisees," which means "separated ones."
d 23:30 As translated from the Hebrew Matthew. The Greek is "We would not have joined them in killing the prophets."
e 23:33 As translated from the Hebrew Matthew.

Jehoiada,[a] whom you killed as he stood in the temple between the brazen altar and the Holy Place. [36]I tell you the truth: the judgment for all these things will fall upon this generation!"

Jesus Prophesies Judgment Coming to Jerusalem

[37]"O Jerusalem, Jerusalem—you are the city that murders your prophets! You are the city that stones the very messengers who were sent[b] to deliver you! So many times I have longed to gather a wayward people, as a hen gathers her chicks under her wings—but you were too stubborn to let me. [38]And now it is too late, since your city will be left in ruins.[c] [39]For you will not see me again until you are able to say, 'We welcome the one who comes to us in the name of the Lord.'"[d]

---

a 23:35 As translated from the Hebrew Matthew. See 2 Chronicles 24:20–21. This strengthens the argument that the original manuscript of Matthew was written in Hebrew. The Greek erroneously lists Zechariah's father as Barachiah. There was indeed a Zechariah son of Barachiah, but he didn't live until after the crucifixion of Christ and was killed in a massacre of AD 69 by zealots inside the temple. See Sabine Baring-Gould, *The Lost and Hostile Gospels* (Williams & Norgate, 1874), 138. It is also recorded by the Jewish historian Josephus that Zechariah was the son of Jehoiada. *B. J.* 4.6.4. Furthermore, Jerome, in his commentary on Matthew, says, "In the [Hebrew] Gospel [of Matthew] which the Nazarenes use, for 'son of Barachiah' we find written, 'son of Jehoiada.'" Quoted from http://www.textexcavation.com/nazoraeangospel.html.
b 23:37 Or "apostles (sent ones)."
c 23:38 See Jeremiah 12:7 and 22:5.
d 23:39 See Psalm 118:26.

Twenty-four

Jesus Prophesies the Destruction of the Temple

¹As Jesus was leaving the temple courts, his disciples came to him and pointed out the beautiful aspects of the architecture of the temple structures. ²And Jesus turned to them and said, **"Take a good look at all these things, for I'm telling you, there will not be one stone left upon another. It will all be leveled!"**[a]

³Later, when they arrived at the Mount of Olives, his disciples came privately to where he was sitting and said, "Tell us, when will these things happen? And what supernatural sign should we expect to signal your coming and the completion of this age?"[b]

⁴Jesus answered, **"At that time deception will run rampant. So beware that you are not fooled! ⁵For many will appear on the scene claiming my authority or saying about themselves, 'I am God's Anointed,' and they will lead many astray.**

⁶**"You will hear of wars nearby and revolutions on every side, with more rumors of wars to come. Don't panic or give in to your fears, for the breaking apart of the world's systems is destined to happen. But it won't yet be the end; it will still be unfolding.**

⁷**"Nations**[c] **will go to war against each other and kingdom against kingdom. And there will be terrible earthquakes—seismic events of epic**

---

a 24:2 This prophecy of Jesus was fulfilled by the Roman prince Titus, who, in the Roman war of AD 67–70, destroyed the temple. In about AD 135 the emperor Hadrian completely destroyed the city of Jerusalem and built a new city on its foundations and named it Elia Helipolis.

b 24:3 Although it is possible to translate this "the end of the world," the Hebraic mind-set of the end of days is a transition into a new age of the Messiah's coming that would restore all things.

c 24:7 Or "ethnic group." See 2 Chronicles 15:6 and Isaiah 19:2.

proportion, horrible epidemics[a] and famines in place after place. [8]This is how the first contractions and birth pains of the new age will begin!"[b]

Persecution of Believers

[9]"You can expect to be persecuted, even killed; for you will be hated by all the nations because of your love for me.[c] [10]Then many will stop following me and fall away,[d] and they will betray one another and hate one another. [11]And many lying prophets will arise, deceiving multitudes and leading them away from the path of truth. [12]There will be such an increase of sin and lawlessness that those whose hearts once burned with passion for God and others will grow cold. [13]But keep your hope[e] to the end and you will experience life and deliverance.

[14]"Yet through it all, this joyful assurance of the realm of heaven's kingdom will be proclaimed all over the world, providing every nation with a demonstration of the reality of God. And after this the end of this age will arrive."

The Detestable Idol that Brings Misery

[15]"When you witness what Daniel prophesied, 'the disgusting destroyer,'[f] taking its stand[g] in the holy place (let the reader learn),[h] [16]then those in

---

a 24:7 Although missing from a few Greek manuscripts, "horrible epidemics" is found in the Hebrew Matthew, the Aramaic, and the majority of Greek texts.

b 24:8 Implied in the context. The translators are aware of distorted use of the words "new age"; however, true believers in Christ anticipate the coming of a new day (age) dawning, with Christ and his bride ruling the nations. See Joel 2 and Revelation 3:21.

c 24:9 Or "because of my name."

d 24:10 The Aramaic is "Many will stumble (or take offence)."

e 24:13 As translated from the Aramaic. The Greek is "endure."

f 24:15 Or "the abomination (sin) that brings desolation (desecration)." See Daniel 8:13, 9:27, 11:31, and 12:11. Jesus is saying that Daniel's prophecy was not yet fulfilled in Jesus' time. Many see the fulfillment of this prophecy in AD 70, when Titus, the Roman prince, went into the temple and sacrificed animals to Jupiter.

g 24:15 The Aramaic is "the defiling sign of desolation piling up (setting up) in the holy place."

h 24:15 These parenthetical words were added by Matthew to encourage us to seek the Lord for the understanding of this mystery. Jesus, speaking in the role of the True Prophet, gives us truth to ponder in veiled language.

the land of Judah must escape to the higher ground.[a] [17]On that day, if you happen to be outside,[b] don't go back inside to gather belongings. [18]And if you're working out in the field, don't run back home to get a coat. [19]It will be especially hard for pregnant women and for those nursing their babies in those days. [20]So pray that your escape will not be during the winter months or on a Sabbath. [21]For this will be a time of great misery beyond the magnitude of anything the world has ever seen or ever will see. Unless God limited those days, no one would escape. [22]But because of his love for those chosen to be his, he will shorten that time of trouble.

[23]"And you will hear reports from some, saying, 'Look, he has returned,' 'The Messiah is over here,' or, 'The Messiah is over there!' Don't believe it. [24]For there will be imposters falsely claiming to be God's 'Anointed One,' and false prophets[c] will arise to perform miracle signs to lead astray, if possible, those God has chosen to be his. [25]Remember this, for I prophesy it will happen! [26]So if someone says to you, 'Look, the Anointed One has returned! He's in the desert,' don't go chasing after him. Or if they say to you, 'Look, he's here in our house,'[d] don't believe it. [27]The appearing of the Son of Man will burst forth with the brightness of a lightning strike that shines from one end of the sky to the other, illuminating the earth. [28]How do birds of prey know where the dead body is?[e] They just know instinctively, and so you will know when I appear."

The Appearing of the Son of Man

[29]"Then immediately this is what will take place: 'The sun will be darkened and the moon give no light. The stars will fall from the sky and all the

---

a 24:16 See Jeremiah 16:16, Zechariah 14:5, and Luke 21:20–22.
b 24:17 Or "on the roof."
c 24:24 The Aramaic is "prophets of lies."
d 24:26 Or "in the inner rooms."
e 24:28 Or "Wherever you find the corpse, there the eagles will gather." This peculiar verse is best understood as a parallel of vultures knowing where the carcass is as an example of how instinctively believers will know when Jesus has appeared.

cosmic powers will be shaken.'[a] [30]Then the sign announcing the Son of Man will appear in the sky, and all the nations of the earth will mourn over him.[b] And they will see the Son of Man appearing in the clouds of heaven, revealed with mighty power,[c] great splendor, and glory. [31]And he will send his messengers with the loud blast of the trumpet,[d] and with a great voice[e] they will gather his beloved chosen ones by the four winds, from one end of heaven to the other!"

A Parable of the Fig Tree

[32]"Now learn the lesson from the parable of the fig tree. When spring arrives and it sends out its tender branches and sprouts leaves, you know that ripe fruit[f] is soon to appear. [33]So it will be with you, for when you observe all these things taking place, you will know that he is near, even at the door! [34]I assure you, the end of this age will not come until all I have spoken comes to pass. [35]The earth and sky will wear out and fade away before one word I speak loses its power or fails to accomplish its purpose."

Live Always Ready for His Appearing

[36]"Concerning that day and exact hour, no one knows when it will arrive, not even the angels of heaven[g]—only the Father knows. [37]For it will be

---

a 24:29 See Isaiah 13:10, Isaiah 34:4, Joel 2:10, and Amos 8:9. This can also be viewed as a Hebraic metaphor of the lights of the natural realm being shut off and replaced with heaven's glory. Lights out on the old order. Sun, moon, and stars are also representative of the governmental structures failing with great calamity. A new order, a new glory, is coming to replace the fading glories of this world.

b 24:30 See Zechariah 12:10–14 and Revelation 1:7.

c 24:30 The Hebrew Matthew is "mighty warriors."

d 24:31 There is always a deeper meaning to the literal understanding of the text of the Bible. This deeper meaning does not negate the literal, but gives a fuller comprehension. Clouds are metaphors of God's presence among his people. The trumpet blast is symbolic of the universal announcement that will be heard by all.

e 24:31 As translated from the Hebrew Matthew, which can also be translated "with a great shout." This is also found in the Latin Vulgate translated by Jerome, who is believed to have had access to the manuscript of the Hebrew Matthew.

f 24:32 As translated from the Hebrew Matthew. The Greek is "Summer is near."

g 24:36 A few Greek manuscripts add "nor the Son." However, that phrase is missing in many Greek texts and is not found in the Hebrew Matthew, the Aramaic, or the Latin Vulgate.

exactly like it was in the days of Noah when the Son of Man appears. [38]Before the flood, people lived their lives eating, drinking, marrying, and having children.[a] [39]They didn't realize the end was near until Noah entered the ark, and then suddenly, the flood came and took them all away in judgment. It will happen the same way when the Son of Man appears. [40]At that time, two men will be working on the farm; one will be taken away in judgment, the other left. [41]Two women will be grinding grain; one will be taken away in judgment, the other left.[b] [42]This is why you must stay alert: because no one knows the day your Lord will come.

[43]"But realize this: If a homeowner had known what time of night the burglar would come to rob his house, he would have been alert and ready, and not let his house be robbed. [44]So always be ready, alert, and prepared, because at an hour when you're not expecting him, the Son of Man will come."

The Wise and Faithful Servant

[45]"Who is the one qualified to oversee the master's house? He will be a reliable servant who is wise and faithful, one he can depend on. The master will want to give him the responsibility of overseeing others in his house, for his servant will lead them well and give them food at the right time. [46]What joy and blessing will come to that faithful servant when the master comes home to find him serving with excellence! [47]I can promise you, the master will raise him up and put him in charge of all that he owns.

[48]"But the evil servant says in his heart, My master delays his coming, and who knows when he will return? And because of the delay, the

---

a 24:38 As translated from the Hebrew Matthew, which is literally "being fruitful and multiplying (having children)." The Greek is "marrying and giving in marriage."

b 24:41 One of the three manuscripts of the Hebrew Matthew, known as Shem-Tob, includes additional text: "This is because the angels at the end of the age will first remove the stumbling blocks (the wicked) from the world and will separate the good from the evil." This passage is not speaking of what is known as the "rapture," for as it was in the days of Noah, the evil were "taken" and the righteous were "left."

servant mistreats those in his master's household. Instead of caring for the ones he was appointed to serve, ⁴⁹he abuses the other servants and gives himself over to eating and drinking with drunkards. ⁵⁰Let me tell you what will happen to him. His master will suddenly return at a time that surprises him, and he will remove the abusive, selfish servant from his position of trust. ⁵¹And the master will cut him in two[a] and assign him to the place of great sorrow and anguish[b] along with all the other pretenders and unbelievers."

---

a 24:51 Most likely hyperbole. The Greek word *dichotomeō* could also mean that God "will separate him from himself (soul and body)."
b 24:51 Or "gnashing of teeth."

Twenty-five

A Parable about Ten Virgins

[1]"At the time my coming draws near, heaven's kingdom realm can be compared to ten maidens who took their oil lamps and went outside to meet the bridegroom and his bride.[a] [2-4]Five of them were foolish and ill-prepared, for they took no extra[b] oil for their lamps. Five of them were wise and sensible, for they took flasks of olive oil with their lamps. [5]When the bridegroom didn't come when they expected, they all grew drowsy and fell asleep. [6]Then suddenly, in the middle of the night, they were awakened by the shout 'Get up! The bridegroom is here! Come out and welcome him!' [7]So all the girls got up and trimmed their lamps. [8]But the foolish ones were running out of oil, so they said to the five wise ones, 'Share your oil with us, because our lamps are going out!'

[9]"'We can't,' they replied. 'We don't have enough for all of us. You'll have to go and buy some for yourselves!'

[10]" While the five girls were out buying oil, the bridegroom appeared. Those who were ready and waiting were escorted inside with him and the wedding party to enjoy the feast. And then the door was locked. [11]Later, the five foolish girls came running up to the door and pleaded, 'Lord, Lord, let us come in!'

---

a 25:1 As translated from the Hebrew Matthew and a few Greek manuscripts. Most Greek manuscripts have only "bridegroom." This would mean the ten virgins were going to marry one man, a doubtful teaching from Jesus. The ten virgins were bridesmaids, ladies-in-waiting. This was not Jesus condoning polygamy. It is possible that the parable hints of Zechariah 8:23.

b 25:2–4 Implied in the context. See verse 8. Oil in the Scriptures is a metaphor of the Holy Spirit, who brings us revelation of the Word of God and power for ministry.

[12]"But he called back, 'Go away! Do I know you? I can assure you, I don't even know you!'

[13]"That is the reason you should always stay awake and be alert, because you don't know the day or hour when the Bridegroom will appear."[a]

A Parable about Financial Stewardship

[14]"Again, heaven's kingdom realm is like the wealthy man who went on a long journey and summoned all his trusted servants and assigned his financial management over to them. [15]Before he left on his journey, he entrusted a bag of five thousand gold coins to one of his servants, to another a bag of two thousand gold coins, and to the third a bag of one thousand gold coins, each according to his ability to manage.[b]

[16]"The one entrusted with five thousand gold coins immediately went out and traded with the money, and he doubled his investment. [17]In the same way, the one who was entrusted with two thousand gold coins traded with the sum and likewise doubled his investment. [18]But the one who had been entrusted with one thousand gold coins dug a hole in the ground and buried his master's money.

[19]"After much time had passed, the master returned to settle accounts with his servants. [20]The one who was entrusted with five thousand gold coins came and brought ten thousand, saying, 'See, I have doubled your money.'

[21]"Commending his servant, the master replied, 'You have done well, and proven yourself to be my loyal and trustworthy servant. Because you have been a faithful steward to manage a small sum, now I will put you in charge of much, much more. You will experience the delight of your master, who will say to you, "Come celebrate with me!"'

a 25:13 As translated from the Hebrew Matthew.
b 25:15 Or "five talents...two talents...one talent." A talent, although hard to determine exactly how much it represents, is a measure of weight. King Solomon received 666 talents of gold as his yearly tribute. A talent is clearly a large sum of money. See 2 Chronicles 9:13 and 1 Kings 10:14.

²²"Then the one who had been entrusted with two thousand gold coins came in and said, 'See, my master, I have doubled what you have entrusted to me.'

²³"Commending his servant, the master replied, 'You have done well, and proven yourself to be my loyal and trustworthy servant. Because you were faithful to manage a small sum, now I will put you in charge of much, much more. You will experience the delight of your master, who will say to you, "Come celebrate with me!"'

²⁴"Then the one who had been entrusted with one thousand gold coins came to his master and said, 'Look, sir. I know that you are a hard man to please and you're a shrewd and ruthless businessman who grows rich on the backs of others.ᵃ ²⁵I was afraid of you, so I went and hid your money and buried it in the ground. But here it is— take it, it's yours.'

²⁶"Angered by what he heard, the master said to him, 'You're an untrustworthyᵇ and lazy servant! If you knew I was a shrewd and ruthless business man who always makes a profit, why didn't you deposit my money in the bank? ²⁷Then I would have received it all back with interest when I returned.ᶜ ²⁸But because you were unfaithful, I will take the one thousand gold coins and give them to the one who has ten thousand. ²⁹For the one who has will be given more, until he overflows with abundance. And the one with hardly anything, even what little he has will be taken from him.'ᵈ

---

a 25:24 Or "that you harvest where you didn't sow and gather where you didn't plant." This is most likely a proverb, a figure of speech that reinforces the thought of the servant that his master was strict, harsh, and ruthless. The attitude of the servant was "You are so ruthless, you're like a man who expects a harvest from a field he didn't plant!"

b 25:26 Or "evil."

c 25:27 The Aramaic can be translated "Why didn't you throw my money into the offering? Then I would have returned to ask for what was mine together with its bounty." The implication is that money given in sacred offering to God will be returned with even more, by God's generosity. See Luke 6:38.

d 25:29 By implication the parable is stating, "The one who has (a heart of faithful stewardship) will be given more (to manage). And the one who has very little (faithfulness, wisdom, integrity) will lose the little he has (failed to manage well)."

[30]"Then the master said to his other servants, 'Now, throw that good-for-nothing servant far away from me into the outer darkness, where there will be great misery and anguish!'"

The Judgment of the Multitudes

[31]"When the Son of Man appears in his majestic glory, with all his angels by his side, he will take his seat on his throne of splendor, [32]and all the nations will be gathered together before him.[a] And like a shepherd who separates the sheep from the goats, he will separate all the people. [33]The 'sheep' he will put on his right side and the 'goats' on his left. [34]Then the King will turn to those on his right and say, 'You have a special place in my Father's heart. Come and experience the full inheritance of the kingdom realm that has been destined for you from before the foundation[b] of the world! [35]For when you saw me hungry, you fed me. When you found me thirsty, you gave me something to drink. When I had no place to stay, you invited me in, [36]and when I was poorly clothed, you covered me. When I was sick, you tenderly cared for me, and when I was in prison you visited me.'

[37]"Then the godly will answer him, 'Lord, when did we see you hungry or thirsty and give you food and something to drink? [38]When did we see you with no place to stay and invite you in? When did we see you poorly clothed and cover you? [39]When did we see you sick and tenderly care for you, or in prison and visit you?'

[40]"And the King will answer them, 'Don't you know? When you cared for one of the least important of these my little ones, my true brothers and sisters, you demonstrated love for me.'

[41]"Then to those on his left the King will say, 'Leave me! For you are under the curse of eternal fire that has been destined for the devil and all his demons. [42]For when you saw me hungry, you refused to give me food,

a 25:32 See Daniel 7:13–14.
b 25:34 Or "from before the fall of the world."

and when you saw me thirsty, you refused to give me something to drink. [43]I had no place to stay, and you refused to take me in as your guest. When you saw me poorly clothed, you closed your hearts and would not cover me. When you saw that I was sick, you didn't lift a finger to help me, and when I was imprisoned, you never came to visit me.'

[44]"And then those on his left will say, 'Lord, when did we see you hungry or thirsty and not give you food and something to drink? When did we see you homeless, or poorly clothed? When did we see you sick and not help you, or in prison and not visit you?'

[45]"Then he will answer them, 'Don't you know? When you refused to help one of the least important among these my little ones, my true brothers and sisters, you refused to help and honor me.' [46]And they will depart from his presence and go into eternal punishment. But the godly and beloved 'sheep' will enter into eternal bliss."

Twenty-six

Jesus Prophesies His Crucifixion

[1]After Jesus had completed his teachings, he said to his disciples, [2]**"You know that the Feast of the Passover begins in two more days. That's when the Son of Man is to be betrayed and handed over to be crucified."**

[3]Meanwhile, the prominent priests and religious leaders of the nation were gathered in the palace of the high priest Caiaphas.[a] [4]That's when they made their decision to secretly[b] have Jesus captured and killed. [5]But they all agreed, "We can't do this during the Passover celebrations or we could have a riot on our hands."

A Woman Anoints Jesus

[6-7]Then Jesus went to Bethany, to the home of Simon, a man Jesus had healed of leprosy. A woman came into the house, holding an alabaster flask[c] filled with fragrant and expensive oil.[d] She walked right up to Jesus, and in a lavish gesture of devotion,[e] she poured out the costly oil, and it

---

a 26:3 Caiaphas was a Sadducee with political connections to Pilate's government. He was the son-in-law of Annas, who had been deposed from his office by the Roman procurator Valerious, but he was still viewed by the people as the high priest. In effect, Israel had two high priests at the same time, Annas and Caiaphas, thus violating Jewish law.

b 26:4 Or "deceitfully" (Aramaic, "with false testimony").

c 26:6–7 Jars such as this usually had a long neck that would be broken off and the oil poured out. The woman is identified as Mary, the sister of Lazarus and Martha. See Song of Solomon 1:12, Mark 14:3, Luke 7:37, and John 12:1–5.

d 26:6–7 This was spikenard (or nard), a spice taken from a plant that grows in northern India near the Himalayas. This costly perfume would have been carried over land to the Middle East. Many believe this jar of spikenard would have cost the average worker a year's wages. It was a common practice among the Jews to prepare a body for burial with fragrant ointment.

e 26:6-7 Implied in the text.

cascaded over his head as he was at the table. [8]When the disciples saw this, they were offended. "What a total waste!" they grumbled. "We could have sold it for a great deal of money and given it to the poor."

[10]Jesus knew their thoughts and said to them, **"Why are you critical of this woman? She has done a beautiful act of kindness for me. [11]You will always have someone poor whom you can help, but you will not always have me. [12]When she poured the fragrant oil over me, she was preparing my body for burial.**[a] **[13]I promise you that as this wonderful gospel spreads all over the world, the story of her lavish devotion to me will also be mentioned in memory of her."**[b]

Judas Agrees to Betray Jesus

[14]One of the twelve apostles, Judas the locksmith,[c] went to the leading priests [15]and said, "How much are you willing to pay me to betray Jesus into your hands?" They agreed to pay him thirty silver coins.[d] [16]Immediately Judas began to scheme and look for an opportunity to betray him.

Jesus Celebrates Passover with His Disciples

[17]On the first day of Passover,[e] the day when any bread made with yeast was removed from every Jewish home, the disciples came to Jesus and

---

a 26:12 It is entirely possible that when the Roman soldiers pierced Jesus' beautiful feet and put the crown of thorns on his lovely head, they could have smelled this fragrant oil.

b 26:13 Jesus' prophecy is that Mary would be included in the gospel account. Her act of devotion is mentioned in three of the four gospels. You can't read the New Testament without knowing of Mary's worship of Jesus.

c 26:14 Or "Judah Iscariot." Iscariot is not his last name or the name of a town. It means "locksmith." *Iscariot* comes from an Aramaic word for "brass lock." The one who held the key to the finances of the twelve disciples brazenly wanted to lock up Jesus.

d 26:15 See Zechariah 11:12–13. Assuming the thirty pieces of silver were tetradrachms, it would represent about four months' wages of a skilled worker. If the coins were the Roman denarius, it would be about five week's wages. If they were Jewish shekels, it would have been a very modest sum. How could anyone put a monetary value on the life of the glorious Son of God?

e 26:17 Or "the first day of Unleavened Bread." The Aramaic reads, "on the day before the Passover festival." This was the first day of an eight-day celebration to commemorate the deliverance of the Hebrew slaves out of Egypt. The Jews would eat a roasted lamb after sunset in a family group of at least ten people. The meal would include bitter herbs (in remembrance of their bitter years of slavery), unleavened bread, and four cups of wine mixed with water. See Numbers 9:2–5.

asked, "Where should we prepare the Passover meal[a] for you?"

[18]He answered them, **"My heart longs with great desire to eat this Passover meal with you.[b] Go into Jerusalem and you will encounter a man.[c] Tell him that the teacher says, 'My appointed time[d] is near. I am coming to your home to eat the Passover meal with my disciples.'"**

[19]The disciples did as Jesus had instructed them, and they prepared the Passover meal. [20]When evening came he took his place at the table and dined with the twelve. [21]While they were eating, Jesus spoke up and said, **"One of you is about to betray me."**

[22]Feeling deeply hurt by these words, one after another asked him, "You don't mean me, do you?"

[23]He answered, **"It is one who has shared meals with me as an intimate friend.[e] [24]All that was prophesied of me will take place, but how miserable it will be for the one who betrays the Son of Man. It would be far better for him if he had never been born!"**

[25]Then finally, Judas the traitor spoke up and asked him, "Teacher,[f] perhaps it is I?"

Jesus answered, **"You said it."**

The Lord's Supper

[26]As they ate, Jesus took the bread and blessed it and broke it and gave it to his disciples. He said to them, **"This is my body. Eat it."** [27]Then taking the

---

a 26:17 That is, "the Passover seder."

b 26:18 As translated from the Hebrew Matthew and other external evidence. The Greek text does not include this sentence; however, it seems to be essentially the same as found in Luke 22:15, which may support the theory that part of Luke's eyewitness accounts may have included Matthew.

c 26:18 The Greek is actually "Mr. So-and-So." This was someone who would know who the teacher was and understand what it meant when Jesus said, "My time is near." The Hebrew Matthew adds this line: "He will volunteer for the task."

d 26:18 An obvious ellipsis that could mean "My time of fulfilling my destiny is near."

e 26:23 Or "he who has dipped his hand with me in the dish." This is a figure of speech of one who was an intimate friend of Jesus. To break bread together was a sign of friendship throughout the Middle East.

f 26:25 Notice that the other eleven disciples called Jesus "Lord." Judas called him "teacher."

cup of wine and giving praises to the Father, he entered into covenant with them,[a] saying, **"This is my blood. Each of you must drink it in fulfillment of the covenant. 28For this is the blood that seals the new covenant.[b] It will be poured out for many for the complete forgiveness of sins. 29The next time we drink this, I will be with you and we will drink it together with a new understanding in the kingdom realm of my Father."[c]**

30Then they sang a psalm[d] and left for the Mount of Olives.

Jesus Prophesies Peter's Denial

31Along the way Jesus said to them, **"Before the night is over, you will all desert me. This will fulfill the prophecy of the Scripture that says:**

> **I will strike down the shepherd**
> **And all the sheep will scatter far and wide![e]**

32**"But after I am risen, I will go ahead of you to Galilee and will meet you there."[f]**

33Then Peter spoke up and said, "Even if all the rest lose their faith and fall away, I will still be beside you, Jesus!"

34**"Are you sure, Peter?"** Jesus said. **"In fact, before the rooster crows a few hours from now, you will have denied me three times."**

---

a 26:27 As translated from the Aramaic.

b 26:28 The Aramaic word *khawdata* can be translated "new," but is better rendered "renewed covenant" or "repaired covenant." See Leviticus 17:11 and Jeremiah 31:31–37. After each disciple took the cup and drank from it, they passed it to the next one. This was a love covenant between Jesus and each of his disciples, and it sealed the affection they would have for one another.

c 26:29 We are now in the realm of the kingdom of God. The Holy Spirit brings us into the body of Christ and into the reality of the kingdom of God. It is growing and increasing in scope, and every time believers drink of the cup of communion, Jesus is present with us. It is the Lord's table, not ours. This was a prophecy of what would happen in just a matter of days from then, as believers would break bread together in remembrance of what Jesus did for each one of us. See Acts 2:42. Jesus now drinks it with us in a new way, and not just once a year at Passover, but every time we worship him by taking communion.

d 26:30 Or "a hymn." The Aramaic is "They offered praise." It was the custom after celebrating the Passover seder to conclude with singing one of the Hallel psalms (115–118).

e 26:31 See Zechariah 13:7.

f 26:32 As translated from the Hebrew Matthew.

³⁵Peter replied, "I absolutely will never deny you, even if I have to die with you!" And all the others said the same thing.

Jesus Prays in Gethsemane

³⁶Then Jesus led his disciples to an orchard called "The Oil Press."[a] He told them, **"Sit here while I go and pray over there."** ³⁷He took Peter, James, and John with him.[b] However, an intense feeling of great sorrow plunged his soul into deep sorrow and agony. ³⁸And he said to them, **"My heart is overwhelmed and crushed with grief. It feels as though I'm dying. Stay here and keep watch with me."**

³⁹Then he walked a short distance away, and overcome with grief, he threw himself facedown on the ground and prayed, **"My Father, if there is any way you can deliver me from this suffering,**[c] **please take it from me. Yet what I want is not important, for I only desire to fulfill your plan for me."** Then an angel from heaven appeared to strengthen him.[d]

⁴⁰Later, he came back to his three disciples and found them all sound asleep. He awakened Peter and said to him, **"Do you lack the strength to stay awake with me for even just an hour? ⁴¹Keep alert and pray that you'll**

---

a 26:36 Or "Gethsemane," which means "oil press." This was located on the lower slope of the Mount of Olives near the brook Kidron. King David left Jerusalem weeping as he crossed the Kidron Valley and up the Mount of Olives (2 Samuel 15:23). Now the Son of David comes into that valley with great sorrow on his way into Jerusalem to be crucified. Kidron comes from the Hebrew verb *qadar*, which means "to grow dark" or "to mourn."

b 26:37 Or "Peter and the two sons of Zebedee."

c 26:39 Or "If possible, take away this cup of suffering." The cup becomes a metaphor of the great suffering that Jesus had to drink that night in the garden. However, Jesus was not asking the Father for a way around the cross. Rather, he was asking God to keep him alive through this night of suffering so that he could carry the cross and take away our sins. According to the prophecies of the Old Testament, Jesus was to be pierced on a cross. We learn from Hebrews 5:7 that Jesus' prayer was answered that night as the cup was indeed taken from him. An angel of God came to strengthen him and deliver him from premature death. The "cup" he was asking God to let pass from him was the cup of premature death that Satan was trying to make him drink in the garden, not the death he would experience the next day on the cross. He had already sweat drops of blood, but the prophecies had to be fulfilled of being pierced on a cross for our transgressions. God answered his cry and he lived through the agony of Gethsemane so that he could be our sacrifice for sin on Calvary. Jesus did not waver in the garden. We have a brave Savior.

d 26:39 As translated from the Hebrew Matthew. See Luke 22:43, which may be evidence of Luke having access to the Hebrew Matthew account.

be spared from this time of testing. You should have learned by now that your spirit is eager enough, but your humanity is weak."[a]

⁴²Then he left them for a second time to pray in solitude. *He said to God,* "My Father, if there is not a way that you can deliver me from this suffering,[b] then your will must be done."

⁴³He came back to the disciples and found them sound asleep, for they couldn't keep their eyes open. ⁴⁴So he left them and went away to pray the same prayer for the third time.

⁴⁵When he returned again to his disciples, he awoke them, saying, **"Are you still sleeping and resting? Don't you know the hour has come for the Son of Man to be handed over to the authority of sinful men? ⁴⁶Get up and let's go, for the betrayer has arrived."**

The Betrayal and Arrest of Jesus

⁴⁷At that moment Judas, his once-trusted disciple, appeared, along with a large crowd of men armed with swords and clubs. They had been sent to arrest Jesus by order of the ruling priests and Jewish religious leaders. ⁴⁸Now, Judas, the traitor, had arranged to give them a signal that would identify Jesus, for he had told them, "Jesus is the one whom I will kiss. So grab him!"

⁴⁹Judas quickly stepped up to Jesus and said, "Shalom, Rabbi," and he kissed him *on both cheeks.*[c]

⁵⁰**"My beloved friend,"**[d] Jesus said, **"is this why you've come?"**[e]

Then the armed men seized Jesus to arrest him. ⁵¹But one of the disciples[f] pulled out a dagger and swung it at the servant of the high priest, slashing off his ear. ⁵²Jesus said to him, **"Put your dagger away. For all those**

---

a 26:41 The Aramaic is "The flesh is failing."
b 26:42 See footnote for verse 39 and Hebrews 5:7.
c 26:49 This would have been the customary kiss among the Jews of that day.
d 26:50 As translated from the Hebrew Matthew.
e 26:50 As translated from the Aramaic. The Greek is "Do what you've come to do."
f 26:51 From John 18:10 we learn that the disciple was Peter. Matthew, although knowing it was his friend Peter, kept him from any embarrassment by not naming him in his gospel narrative.

who embrace violence will die by violence.[a] [53]Don't you realize that I could ask my heavenly Father for angels to come at any time to deliver me? And instantly he would answer me by sending twelve armies of the angelic host[b] to come and protect us. [54]But that would thwart the prophetic plan of God. For it has been written that it would happen this way."

[55]Then Jesus turned to the mob and said, "Why would you arrest me with swords and clubs as though I were an outlaw? Day after day I sat in the temple courts with you, teaching the people, yet you didn't arrest me. [56]But all of this fulfills the prophecies of the Scriptures."

At that point all of his disciples ran away and abandoned him.

Jesus Is Condemned by the Religious Leaders

[57]Those who arrested Jesus led him away to Caiaphas, the chief priest, and to a meeting where the religious scholars and the supreme Jewish council were already assembled.[c] [58]Now, Peter had followed the mob from a distance all the way to the chief priest's courtyard. And after entering, he sat with the servants[d] of the chief priest who had gathered there, waiting to see how things would unfold. [59]The chief priests and the entire supreme Jewish council of leaders[e] were doing their best to find false charges that they could bring against Jesus, because they were looking for a reason to put him to death.

[60]Many false witnesses came forward, but the evidence could not be corroborated. Finally two men came forward [61]and declared, "This man said, 'I can destroy God's temple and build it again in three days!'"

a 26:52 The Aramaic reads, "Those who have taken up swords against me will all die by the sword." The Aramaic is a prophecy that those armed men who came against Jesus in the garden that night would die by the sword.

b 26:53 Or "twelve legions." A legion was a detachment of six thousand Roman soldiers. Jesus could have called down seventy-two thousand angels to come to his aid. The number twelve was a reminder to the twelve disciples that God had more than enough protection for them all.

c 26:57 Or "elders." The supreme Jewish council (Sanhedrin) is made explicit in verse 59.

d 26:58 The Aramaic is "temple ushers."

e 26:59 Or "Sanhedrin (or, Great Sanhedrin)," which was a council of seventy men who were appointed to serve as the leadership of the Jewish community and the affairs of the temple.

⁶²Then the chief priest stood up and said to Jesus, "Have you nothing to say about these allegations? Is what they're saying about you true?" ⁶³But Jesus remained silent before them. So the chief priest said to him, "I charge you under oath—in the name of the living God, tell us once and for all if you are the anointed Messiah, the Son of God!"

⁶⁴Jesus answered him, **"You just said it yourself. And more than that, you are about to see the Son of Man seated at the right hand of God, the Almighty.ª And one day you will also see the Son of Man coming in the heavenly clouds!"**

⁶⁵This infuriated the chief priest, and as an act of outrage, he tore his robe and shouted, "What blasphemy! No more witnesses are needed, for you heard this grievous blasphemy." ⁶⁶Turning to the council he said, "Now, what is your verdict?"

"He's guilty and deserves the death penalty!" they answered. ⁶⁷Then they spat on his face and slapped him. Others struck him over and over with their fists. ⁶⁸Then they taunted him by saying, "Oh, Anointed One, prophesy to us! Tell us which one of us is about to hit you next?"

Peter's Denials

⁶⁹Meanwhile, Peter was still sitting outside in the courtyard when a servant girl came up to him and said, "I recognize you. You were with Jesus the Galilean."

⁷⁰In front of everyone Peter denied it and said, "I don't have a clue what you're talking about."

⁷¹Later, as he stood near the gateway of the courtyard, another servant girl noticed him and said, "I know this man is a follower of Jesus the Nazarene!"

---

a 26:64 See Daniel 7:13 and Psalm 110:2.

⁷²Once again, Peter denied it, and with an oath he said, "I tell you, I don't know the man!"

⁷³A short time later, those standing nearby approached Peter and said, "We know you're one of his disciples—we can tell by your speech. Your Galilean accent gives you away!"ᵃ

⁷⁴Peter denied it, and using profanity he said, "I don't know the man!" At that very moment the sound of a crowing rooster pierced the night. ⁷⁵Then Peter remembered the prophecy of Jesus, "Before the rooster crows you will have denied me three times." With a shattered heart, Peter went out of the courtyard, sobbing with bitter tears.

a 26:73 Peter, being from Capernaum in Galilee, spoke the northern dialect of Aramaic, while the people of Jerusalem spoke the southern dialect (Chaldean).

Twenty-seven

Jesus Condemned by the Religious Leaders

[1]Before dawn that morning, all the chief priests and religious leaders resolved to take action against Jesus and decided that he should be executed. [2]So they bound him with chains and led him away to Pilate, the Roman governor.

Judas Commits Suicide

[3]Now, when Judas, the betrayer, saw that Jesus had been sentenced to death, remorse filled his heart. He returned the thirty pieces of silver to the chief priests and religious leaders, [4]saying, "I have sinned because I have betrayed an innocent[a] man."

They replied, "Why are you bothering us? That's your problem."

[5]Then Judas flung the silver coins inside the temple and went out and hanged himself.

[6]The chief priests, picking up the pieces of silver, said, "We can't keep this, for it's unlawful to put blood money into the temple treasury." [7]So after some deliberation, they decided to purchase the potter's field *of clay,*[b] to use as a cemetery for burying strangers. [8]That's why that land has been called "The Field of Blood." [9]This fulfilled the prophecy of Zechariah:[c]

---

a 27:4 The Aramaic word for "innocent," *zakaia,* can also mean "victorious."

b 27:7 Implied in the text and the historical context. This was the field owned by a potter, used for making clay vessels.

c 27:9 As translated from the Hebrew Matthew. See Zechariah 11:12–13. The Greek manuscripts incorrectly identify the prophecy as from Jeremiah. There is no clear prophecy found in Jeremiah that is quoted here by Matthew. The Aramaic reads simply, "spoken of by the prophet." The Hebrew Matthew correctly states, "spoken through Zechariah."

They took the thirty pieces of silver,
The price at which he was valued
By the people of Israel,
The price of a precious man,*a*
¹⁰And with the silver they bought the potter's field,
As the Lord directed.*b*

Jesus Brought before Pilate

¹¹As Jesus stood in front of the Roman governor, Pilate asked him, "So, you are really the king of the Jews?"

Jesus answered, **"You have just spoken it."** ¹²Then he was slandered and accused by the chief priests and religious leaders, but he remained silent.

¹³Pilate said, "Don't you hear these allegations?" ¹⁴But Jesus offered no defense to any of the charges, much to the great astonishment of Pilate.

¹⁵Now, every year at Passover it was the custom of the governor to pardon a prisoner and release him to the people—anyone they wanted. ¹⁶And at that time, Pilate was holding in custody a notorious criminal named Jesus Barabbas.*c* ¹⁷So as the crowds of people assembled outside of Pilate's residence, he went out and offered them a choice. He asked them, "Who would you want me to release to you today, Jesus who is called Barabbas, or Jesus who is called the Anointed One?" ¹⁸(Now, Pilate was fully aware that the religious leaders had handed Jesus over to him because of their bitter jealousy.)

¹⁹Just then, as Pilate was presiding over the tribunal,*d* his wife sent him

a 27:9 As translated from the Aramaic.
b 27:10 Or "as the Lord directed me."
c 27:16 As translated from the Hebrew Matthew and a few Greek manuscripts. Most Greek texts have only Barabbas. The name Barabbas is Aramaic and means "son of a father" or "son who is like his father." He becomes a picture of every son of Adam, our father. Some believe this is a figure of speech, a nickname for one who was born an illegitimate son, with no known father. The true Son of the Father was crucified that day.
d 27:19 Or "sat on the judgment seat."

an urgent message: "Don't harm that holy man,[a] for I suffered a horrible nightmare last night about him!"

[20]Meanwhile, the chief priest and the religious leaders were inciting the crowd to ask for Barabbas to be freed and to have Jesus killed. [21]So Pilate asked them again, "Which of the two men would you like me to release for you?"

They shouted, "Barabbas."

[22]Pilate asked them, "Then what would you have me to do with Jesus who is called the Anointed One?"

They all shouted back, "Crucify him!"

[23]"Why?" Pilate asked. "What has he done wrong?"

But they kept shouting out, "Crucify him!"

Jesus Condemned to Death

[24]When Pilate realized that a riot was about to break out and that it was useless to try to reason with the crowd, he sent for a basin of water. After washing his hands[b] in front of the people, he said, "I am innocent of the blood of this righteous man.[c] The responsibility for his death is now yours!"[d]

[25]And the crowd replied, "Let his blood be on us and on our children!"

[26]So he released Barabbas to the people. He ordered that Jesus be beaten with a whip made of leather straps embedded with metal, and afterward be crucified. [27]Then the guards took him into their military compound, where a detachment of nearly six hundred soldiers surrounded him.

[28]They stripped off his clothing and placed a scarlet robe on him to make fun of him. [29]Then they braided a crown of thorns and set it on his

a 27:19 As translated from the Aramaic.
b 27:24 See Deuteronomy 21:6–7.
c 27:24 As translated from the Hebrew Matthew and the Aramaic.
d 27:24 The Aramaic is "You do as you please!"

head. After placing a reed staff in his right hand, they knelt down before him and irreverently mocked him, saying, "Hail, king of the Jews!" ³⁰Then they spat in his face and took the reed staff from his hand and hit him repeatedly on his head, driving the crown of thorns deep into his brow.ᵃ ³¹When they finished ridiculing him, they took off the scarlet robe and put his own clothes back on him and led him away to be crucified. ³²And as they came out of the city, they stopped an African man named Simon, from Libya,ᵇ and compelled him to carry the cross for Jesus.

The Crucifixion

³³They brought Jesus to Golgotha, which means "Skull Hill."ᶜ ³⁴And there the soldiers offered him a mild painkiller, a drink of wine mixed with gall,ᵈ but after tasting it, he refused to drink it.

³⁵Then they crucified Jesus, nailing his hands and feet to the cross. The soldiers divided his clothing among themselves by rolling dice to see who would win them. ³⁶And the soldiers stood there to watch what would happen and to keep guard over him. ³⁷Above his head they placed a sign that read, "This is Jesus of Nazareth,ᵉ King of Israel."

³⁸Two criminals were also crucified with Jesus, one on each side of

a 27:30 Implied in the context.
b 27:32 Or "from Cyrene," which is present-day Tripoli, Lybia.
c 27:33 The Aramaic word Golgatha is, in Latin, *calvaria*, or Calvary. David brought Goliath's head (Goliath and Golgatha are taken from the same root word) and buried it outside of Jerusalem. Some believe this is where it got its name, Golgatha (the place of the skull). The cross has to pierce the place of the skull for our minds to submit to the revelation of the cross.
d 27:34 See Psalm 69:21.
e 27:37 As translated from the Hebrew Matthew. See John 19:20. Aramaic was the language of the common people in Israel. Hebrew ceased to be their spoken language after 450 BC, after the Jews returned from Babylon. Aramaic remained the language of Israel for nearly one thousand years. Latin was the official language of the Roman Empire. The inscription was also in Greek, for the Alexandrian Jews who had come to observe the Passover in Jerusalem would be unable to read Aramaic. The words were "Jesus, the Nazarene, King of the Jews." The first letters of each of the four words written on the sign in Aramaic (Hebrew) were Y-H-W-H (*Y'shua Hanozri Wumelech ayehudim*). To write these letters, YHWH (also known as the Tetragrammaton), was the Hebrew form of writing the sacred name "Yahweh." No wonder the chief priests were so offended by this sign and insisted that Pilate change it. This was a sign given to Israel, for over Jesus' head on the cross was written "Y-H-W-H! God, the Savior, bled to death for you."

him.[a] [39]And those who passed by shook their heads and spitefully ridiculed him, [40]saying, "We heard you boast that you could destroy the temple and rebuild it in three days! Why don't you save yourself now? If you're really God's Son, come down from the cross!"

[41]Even the ruling priests, with the Jewish scholars and religious leaders, joined in the mockery[b] [42]and kept on saying, "He saved others, but he can't even save himself! Israel's king, is he? He should pull out the nails and come down from the cross right now; then we'll believe in him! [43]He says he puts all his trust in God, so let's see if it's true, and see if God really wants to rescue his 'favorite son'!"[c]

[44]Even the two criminals who were crucified with Jesus began to taunt him, hurling their insults on him.

The Death of the Savior

[45]For three hours, beginning at noon, darkness came over the earth.[d] [46]And at three o'clock Jesus shouted with a mighty voice in Aramaic, **"Eli, Eli, lema sabachthani?"**[e]—that is, **"My God, My God, why have you deserted me?"**[f] [47]Some who were standing near the cross misunderstood and said, "He's calling for Elijah." [48]One bystander ran and got a sponge, soaked it with sour wine, then put it on a stick and held it up for Jesus to drink. [49]But the rest said, "Leave him alone! Let's see if Elijah comes to rescue him."[g]

[50]Jesus passionately cried out,[h] *took his last breath*, and gave up his spirit.

---

a 27:38 See Isaiah 53:12.
b 27:41 See Psalm 22:17, Psalm 109:25, and Lamentations 2:15.
c 27:43 As translated from the Aramaic. See also Psalm 22:8.
d 27:45 Or "the land."
e 27:46 The last words of Jesus were spoken in Aramaic. Every Greek text gives a transliteration of the Aramaic words and then translates them back into Greek.
f 27:46 See Psalm 22:1 and 42:9.
g 27:49 A few Greek manuscripts have an additional sentence: "A soldier took a lance and pierced him in the side and blood and water poured out." It is not found in the Aramaic and many Greek texts of Matthew. If included, it would mean the soldier took Jesus' life with his lance. However, Jesus said that no man could take his life from him. The evidence is compelling that it was not part of the original text, but was taken from John 19:34 and added here.
h 27:50 See Luke 23:46 and John 19:30 to read the words he shouted out at death.

⁵¹At that moment the veil in the Holy of Holies was torn in two from the top to the bottom. The earth shook violently, rocks were split apart, ⁵²and graves were opened. Then many of the holy ones who had died were brought back to life and came out of their graves. ⁵³And after Jesus' resurrection,ᵃ they were plainly seen by many people walking in Jerusalem.ᵇ

⁵⁴Now, when the Roman military officer and his soldiers witnessed what was happening and felt the powerful earthquake, they were extremely terrified. They said, "There is no doubt, this man was the Son of God!"

⁵⁵Watching from a distance were many of the women who had followed him from Galilee and given him support. ⁵⁶Among them were Mary Magdalene, Mary, the mother of James and Joseph, and the mother of James and John.

The Burial of Jesus

⁵⁷At the end of the day, a wealthy man named Joseph, a follower of Jesus from the village of Ramah,ᶜ ⁵⁸approached Pilate and asked to have custody of the body of Jesus. So Pilate consented and ordered that the body be given to him. ⁵⁹Then Joseph wrapped the body in a shroud of fine linen and placed it in his own unused tomb, which had only recently been cut into the rock. ⁶⁰They rolled a large stone to seal the entrance of the tomb and left.

⁶¹Sitting across from the tomb were Mary Magdalene and the other Marys,ᵈ watching all that took place.

⁶²The next day, the day after Preparation Day for Passover, the chief priests and the "separated ones"ᵉ went together to Pilate. ⁶³They said to

a 27:53 The Aramaic reads, "after their rising."
b 27:53 Perhaps one was Joseph, for he had asked that his bones be buried in the Promised Land. He saw a resurrection coming and didn't want to be left out. See Hebrews 11:22. Jesus' resurrection was so powerful that many were instantly raised back to life again along with him.
c 27:57 As translated from the Aramaic. Ramah (formerly Ramathaim Zophim) was the village of Samuel, situated on a hill overlooking Jerusalem. The Greek is "Joseph of Arimathea." Luke tells us that he was a member of the Sanhedrin. See Luke 23:50–51. It is possible that Joseph may have a lost a son the age of Jesus when Herod killed the infants.
d 27:61 As translated from the Hebrew Matthew. See verse 56 and 28:1.
e 27:62 Or "Pharisees," which means "separated ones."

him, "Our master, we remember that this imposter claimed that he would rise from the dead after three days. ⁶⁴So please, order the tomb to be sealed until after the third day. Seal it so that his disciples can't come and steal the corpse and tell people he rose from the dead. Then the last deception would be worse than the first!"

⁶⁵"I will send soldiers to guard the tomb," Pilate replied. "Go with them and make the tomb as secure as possible." ⁶⁶So they left and sealed the stone,ᵃ and Pilate's soldiers secured the tomb.

---

a 27:66 This official seal, if broken, would bring the death penalty to the offender.

Twenty-eight

The Resurrection of Jesus

¹As the Sabbath was ending, at the first light of dawn on the first day of the week, Mary Magdalene and the other Mary[a] went to take a look at the tomb. ²⁻⁴Suddenly, the earth shook violently beneath their feet as the angel of the Lord Jehovah[b] descended from heaven. Lightning flashed around him and his robe was dazzling white! The guards were stunned and terrified—lying motionless like dead men. Then the angel walked up to the tomb, rolled away the stone, and sat on top of it!

⁵The women were breathless and terrified, until the angel said to them, "There's no reason to be afraid. I know you're here looking for Jesus, who was crucified. ⁶He isn't here—he has risen victoriously,[c] just as he said! Come inside the tomb and see the place where our Lord was lying.[d] ⁷Then run and tell his disciples that he has risen from the dead! I give you his message: "I am going ahead of you in Galilee and you will see me there."[e]

⁸They rushed quickly to tell his disciples, and their hearts were deep in wonder and filled with great joy.

⁹Along the way, Jesus suddenly appeared in front of them and said, **"Rejoice!"**[f] They were so overwhelmed by seeing him that they bowed down and grasped his feet in adoring worship.

---

a 28:1 This was Mary, the mother of James and Joseph. See Mark 16:1 and Luke 24:10.
b 28:2–4 Or "the angel of YHWH," as translated from the Aramaic.
c 28:6 As translated from the Aramaic.
d 28:6 As translated from the Aramaic and some Greek texts.
e 28:7 Or "He is going ahead of you to Galilee and you will see him there. Behold, I have told you!"
f 28:9 Or "Be rejoicing!"

¹⁰Then Jesus said to them, **"Throw off all your fears. Go and tell my brothers**[a] **to go to Galilee. They will find me there."**

The Guards Report What They Witnessed

¹¹After the women left the tomb, a few of the guards went into Jerusalem and told the chief priests everything they had seen and heard. ¹²So the chief priests called a meeting with all the religious leaders and came up with a plan. They bribed the guards with a large sum of money ¹³and told them, "Tell everyone, 'While we were asleep, his disciples came at night and stole his body!' ¹⁴If Pilate finds out about this, don't worry. We'll make sure you don't get blamed." ¹⁵So they took the money and did as they were told. (That is why the story of the guards is still circulated among the Jews to this day.)

The Great Commission

¹⁶Meanwhile, the eleven disciples heard the wonderful news from the women and left for Galilee, to the mountain where Jesus had arranged to meet them. ¹⁷The moment they saw him, they worshipped him, but some still had lingering doubts.

¹⁸Then Jesus came close to them and said, **"All the authority of the universe has been given to me.**[b] ¹⁹**Now go in my authority**[c] **and make disciples of all nations, baptizing them in the name of the Father, the Son, and the Holy Spirit.** ²⁰**And teach them to faithfully follow**[d] **all that I have commanded you. And never forget that I AM with you every day, even to the completion of this age."**

---

a 28:10 What an incredible truth! Believers are now his brothers and sisters. See Hebrews 2:11.
b 28:18 There is a sentence found in the Aramaic that is missing in all but one Greek manuscript, which reads, "As my Father has sent me, so I send you."
c 28:19 Implied in the text.
d 28:20 The Aramaic is "keep" or "guard."

About the Translator

Dr. Brian Simmons is known as a passionate lover of God. After a dramatic conversion to Christ, Brian knew that God was calling him to go to the unreached people of the world and present the gospel of God's grace to all who would listen. With his wife Candice and their three children, he spent nearly eight years in the tropical rain forest of the Darien Province of Panama as a church planter, translator, and consultant. Brian was involved in the Paya-Kuna New Testament translation project. He studied linguistics and Bible translation principles with New Tribes Mission. After their ministry in the jungle, Brian was instrumental in planting a thriving church in New England (U.S.), and now travels full time as a speaker and Bible teacher. He has been happily married to Candice for over forty-two years and is known to boast regularly of his children and grandchildren. Brian and Candice may be contacted at:

brian@passiontranslation.com
Facebook.com/passiontranslation
Twitter.com/tPtBible

For more information about the translation project or any of Brian's books, please visit:

www.thepassiontranslation.com
www.stairwayministries.org